Racing: Indian Style

Charles Curtis

Prepared for Publication by Kitty Frank
Cover Art and Illustrations by Hailey East

Racing: Indian Style
Charles Curtis
Compilation Copyright © 2019 Kitty Frank

All rights reserved. No part of this publication may be reproduced, distributed, or transmitted in any form or by any means, without prior written permission of the publisher.

Published by Kitty Frank
Allen, KS

Prepared for Publication by Kitty Frank

Hailey East, Cover Art/Illustrations

Curtis Becker, Cover Design/Interior Layout
curtisbeckerbooks.com

ISBN: 978-0-578-44592-2

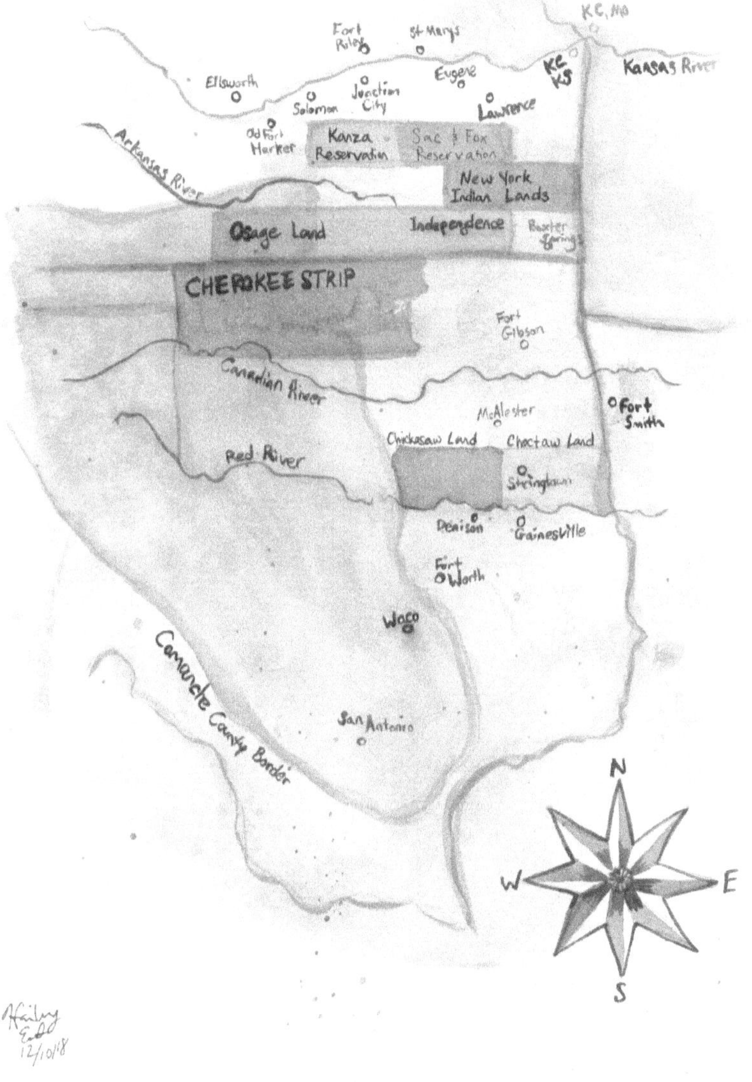
KC, MO
Fort Riley
St Mary's
Kansas River
Ellsworth
Solomon
Junction City
Eugene
KC KS
Lawrence
Old Fort Harker
Kanza Reservation
Sac & Fox Reservation
Arkansas River
New York Indian Lands
Osage Land
Independence
Baxter Springs
CHEROKEE STRIP
Fort Gibson
Canadian River
McAlester
Fort Smith
Chickasaw Land
Choctaw Land
Red River
Stringtown
Denison
Gainesville
Fort Worth
Waco
San Antonio
Comanche County Border
N
W
E
S
12/10/18

DEDICATION

In honor of my favorite retired State Senator and mentor in all things political –

Senator Gerald (Jerry) Karr of the 17th District of Kansas.

      It is because of Jerry's patience during my internship in the 1990 Kansas Legislative session that I learned enough about the day to day work of campaigning, representing and legislating - or as he once referred to it on a bad day as "trying to carry rats in a bucket"- to recognize the importance of this forgotten manuscript.

Statement of Editorial Method

    This is an abridged version of the manuscripts found in the Kansas State Historical Museum Archives in Topeka, Kansas.

    I have prepared this manuscript for an audience of students and general interest readers. With few exceptions all material was transcribed literally. Obvious slips of the pen and errors in typesetting are silently corrected. Spelling and capitalization are the original author's except in cases where it was unclear or cumbersome. In those cases, it has been silently edited to modern usage. When the author's intent is obvious, illegible or missing material, up to five characters in length has been silently provided.

    Edits I have made to the manuscript are in ***bold italic**s*.

THE UNABRIDGED VERSION OF THIS MANUSCRIPT

THE LIFE OF CHARLES CURTIS

The Life of Charles Curtis is another publication by Kitty Frank closely related to this one. It is the unabridged version of this same manuscript by Charles Curtis.

The Life of Charles Curtis is intended for academics and historical researchers. It contains the entire manuscript as found in the archives of the Kansas State Historical Museum. The publication is longer by about 30,000 words and contains more detail and stories about political campaigns, political figures and issues of the time period.

This abridged version, *Racing: Indian Style*, includes only excepts of some articles. The titles notate this. Other articles were omitted entirely without notation. Readers may notice a number in the sequence skipped.

The cover art and map for *The Life of Charles Curtis* were created by Hailey East. It is published through Kindle Direct Publishing and Amazon.com.

STATEMENT REGARDING COPYRIGHT

The current Copyright Law established dates at which Copyright protection for unpublished works expires and those works pass into the public domain. Unpublished works created prior to January 1, 1978, and not published, will pass into the public domain seventy years after the author's death or at the end of 2002, whichever is later. Unpublished works created prior to January 1, 1978, but which are published between then and the end of 2002, will pass into the public domain seventy years after the author's death or at the end of 2047, whichever is later.

I believe these articles were authored by Charles Curtis and remained unpublished throughout his life. Charles died on February 8, 1936. More than seventy years have passed since Charles Curtis' death. If there are legal property violations with my publication, please notify me as soon as possible so I may conform with the original author's written wishes.

The records at the Kansas State Historical Museum Archives in Topeka, Kansas show they received their copy of this manuscript as a donation in 1968 from Mrs. Webster Knight. Charles' youngest daughter, Leona (Mrs. Webster Knight II), passed away in 1965. Her daughter-in-law would also be known as Mrs. Webster Knight (III).

I have been told the Kaw Nation Museum in Kaw City, Oklahoma also has a copy and that family members were given copies at some point long ago.

I first knew of the manuscript's existence after reading **Mixed Bloods and Tribal Dissolution: Charles Curtis and the Quest for Indian Identity** by William E. Unau, University Press of Kansas, 1989. Mr. Unrau lists the typed manuscript as *"Autobiography," William P. Colvin copy, typed copy in the possession of Tom Dennison, Ponca City, Oklahoma.* Charles' sister, Elizabeth, was Mrs. Jerome Colvin.

This was the great crisis of my life. By the action I then took, I would be either white man or Indian for life.

-Charles Curtis

Table of Contents

Article No. I	1
Article No. II	7
Article No. III	19
Article No. IV	35
Article No. V	47
Article No. VI	57
Article No. VII	65
Article No. VIII	75
Article No. IX	83
Article No. X	95
Excerpt from Article No. XII	103
Excerpt from Article No. XIII	111
Excerpt from Article No. XIV	121
Excerpt from Article No. XV	125
Excerpt from Article No. XVII	129
Excerpt from Article No. XIX	131
Excerpt from Article No. XX	135
Excerpt from Article No. XXII	137
About the Author	139

Ellsworth, Kansas, Fall 1870

I shall never forget Ellsworth as I saw it then. The old red-light district which passed with the change in the run of the trail. No one would think of the quiet law-abiding Ellsworth of today as the noisy cattle town of 1869 and 70.

The men found a camping place down by the river and it was not long before there was an 800-yard race matched between Carrie and a Texas horse, which had met all the horses on the trail and had not lost a single race. He had won over the fastest horse in Ellsworth and the cow men, gamblers and members of the sporting fraternity were anxious to get their money up on him. There were a few outside our own crowd; a banker, a lawyer, the suttler of the Fort and the Madam of one of the sporting houses, who backed our horse, but, my grandfather was there and he had plenty of money and took all the bets he could get.

The race was run on a straight track near the river and in the edge of the red light district. There was a large crowd; all the inmates of the sporting houses, all the gamblers, all the cowboys and cattle owners were out. When the time came to take the horses to the starting place, there was but little delay.

The Texas horse was ridden by a young Texas cowboy who weighed about 110 pounds. I rode Carrie and weighed about 70 pounds. Neither of us had saddles. The horses were soon given the word and Carrie led from the start and won the race by three or four lengths. If I had been a rider of experience, I would have won by a length but I was afraid to take a chance and made my mount do her best.

I never knew how much money our crowd won but I know it was a large sum and the gamblers and the madam insisted on taking me to her house and then up town and bought me a new suit of clothes, boots, hat and all and the madam had a new jockey suit made for me. I was proud of my good luck; the suit was a good one. They gave me money and bought me candy and presents and they came to our camp every day.

We could get no more races and soon left. I was anxious to stay. I had never been so petted in my life and I liked it.

Article No. I

In the years when the North American Indian ruled supreme over all of our country there lived west of the Mississippi two strong and powerful tribes of Indians: the Osages and the Kanza (Kansas or Kaw). These tribes had their enemies among the smaller tribes of the Plains but they were dominant over their respective domains until after the Louisiana Purchase by the United States and until the Government began making Treaties with them for the relinquishment of their lands which they held by the right of occupancy. History does not tell us from whence they came but they were in possession and each claimed by the right of occupancy a vast domain which by means of many a hard-fought battle with the other wild tribes of the Plains, they were able to retain.

When the United States became the owner of the lands covered by the Louisiana Purchase, it took the same subject to the rights of the Indians. The Osages occupied lands covering a large part of what is now the states of Missouri, Arkansas, and the southern part of Kansas. The Kansas Indians occupied lands north and west of the Osages and held lands from a little east of the mouth of the Kansas River west into what is now a part of Colorado and north into the state of Nebraska, and claimed a small strip in western Missouri, covering a part of the state in and around what is now known as Independence and Kansas City.

The authorities say that these two tribes were at one time supposed to make up one great tribe as their language and habits are quite similar and they were always friendly. The members intermarried so that many families are of the blood of both tribes.

Charles Curtis

There was an old legend among the Kaws that at one time there had grown up among the Osages a young and mighty leader who was ambitious. He was dissatisfied with the way the older chiefs of the Osages ruled the tribe and he and his followers made a fight against these older in power; he was defeated and he and his followers were driven across the Kansas River and he refused to rejoin the old tribe and he and those who followed and remained with him were given the name of Kanza or Kaw, and they remained as a separate tribe thereafter.

All the old reports of the agents of the French Government and of the Indian Traders and Trappers tell how the British immediately after the Louisiana Purchase sent their trusted half breeds and other agents among the Osages, Kansas and other Indian Tribes who lived within the Purchase, and attempted to win them over to the British but the fact remains that when Lewis and Clark made their historic trip among the western Indian tribes they found the Osages in possession of that section of the country now covered by the State of Missouri, with their main village near the mouth of the Kansas River and they found the Kansas Indians in their village on the Kansas side at the mouth of the Kansas River. It is written that when the Pathfinders visited these two tribes they found them to be friendly to the United States and one report says that as they came in sight of the village of the Kansas Indians, which was on a high bluff or hill on the west side of the Kansas River, where it emptied into the Missouri River, they saw the flag of the United States waving over the wigwam of the head Chief. They reported that they were given a hearty welcome.

In the early days, Pa-hus-ca (now spelled Pawhuska) was the Head Chief of the Osage Tribe of Indians; he was known as White Hair and was a strong man and a great leader of his people. It is claimed that he signed the treaties of 1808, 1815, 1818, 1822 and 1825. He died soon after the signing of the last treaty. After his death and after the tribe was placed on a Reservation in the old Indian Territory, they named the Capitol of their Nation after him. Pawhuska is still the principal town in Osage County, Oklahoma, which covers the lands formerly within the Osage Reservation.

WHITE PLUME (Nom-Pa-Wa-Ra - He who scares all men)
He was born about 1763 and was past seventy years of age when he

died. He was described by Catlin as "A very urbane and hospitable man of good, portly size, speaking some English and making himself good company for all persons who travel through his country and had the good luck to shake his liberal and hospitable hand." Father P. J. De Suit, the Jesuit Missionary, in speaking of White Plume said, "Among the chiefs of this tribe are found men really distinguished in many respects. The most celebrated is White Plume." John I. Irving in his Indian sketches says, "His hair was raven black and his eyes as keen as a hawk's. He was White Plume, Chief of the Kansas Nation."

White Plume was head Chief of the Kansas Tribe of Indians and was one of the ablest and most progressive Indians of his day. He became a warm friend to Lewis and Clark and was of great help to them in their work among the Indians of that section of the country. He was the first Indian Chief for whom the Government built a stone house in the Territory of Kansas.

Charles Curtis

Before White Plume became head Chief of the Kansas Indians he married a daughter of Pawhuska and the oldest daughter of White Plume married Louis Gonvil, a Frenchman who was an Indian trader and a man who had been reared among the Indians of the Plains. As a result of this marriage there were two daughters: Josette and Pelagie Gonvil. After the death of his first wife Louis Gonvil married the second daughter of White Plume, and as a result of this second marriage two children were born: Julie and Victorie Gonvil. These four daughters are mentioned in the Treaty between the United States and the Kansas Indians, made at the city of Saint Louis in 1825, and each of these daughters were given an allotment of one mile of land on the north bank of the Kansas River; Kaw mile four, upon which North Topeka, Kansas, is now located was ceded to Julie Gonvil. These four daughters married French Traders. Julie married Louis Pappan, who had been sent to trade with the Indians of the Plains by the American Fur Company. His people originally came from the North of France to Canada and from there they moved to St. Louis and members of the old Pappan family still live in St. Louis.

After the marriage of Julie Gonvil to Louis Pappan, they built a log house on the north side of her allotment and lived there until they removed to the Kansas Reservation near Council Grove, Kansas. There were seven children born as the result of this marriage, the eldest daughter, Helene Pappan, when old enough was sent to St. Louis to be educated.

In 1821 the Good Ship Elizabeth brought to the New England shores a family of Hubbards who settled in New Hampshire and some of their descendants are still living in the historic old State. One branch of the family moved from New Hampshire to Massachusetts and from there they immigrated to the then new country known as Michigan but after a short stay in that section they were attracted by the interesting stories of the Indian country, and especially by the wonderful accounts of great opportunities that were offered on the Wabash, so they moved to and settled on the banks of that historic river, in what is now known as Vermillion County, Indiana. Some of the family still live in that section of Indiana. Others moved further west and their descendants live in Kansas, Oklahoma, Utah, Oregon, California and other western states. Among the children born in one of the Hubbard families was a daughter, Permelia, who was born at Sheffield, Massachusetts, May 14, 1807, and who died at Topeka, Kansas, September 6th, 1903.

William Curtis was born near Albany, New York, on December 22, 1800, and died in Topeka, Kansas, March 3, 1873. He was a descendant from the Curtis family who came to this country on the ship Lion which landed September 16, 1632. This branch of the family lived in Massachusetts for many years but some members of it moved to New York. About 1805 or 1806 the parents of William Curtis moved to what was then known as the Indian country and settled on the banks of the Wabash in Vermillion County, Indiana.

The Hubbard and Curtis families were pioneers. They helped to settle and develop Indiana in the early days and later on, when the excitement was great over Kansas and when the Kansas and Nebraska question was uppermost in the public mind, they moved to Kansas to help make her free.

In the year 1828 William Curtis and Permelia Hubbard were married and there were fourteen children, seven boys and seven girls, born as the result of this marriage and every one of them lived to manhood and womanhood. William Curtis was a farmer, merchant and boatman and in the earlier days took his own products and those he purchased from his neighbors down the river to New Orleans, where he sold them and returned with such of the products of the south as would be needed and could be used by his neighbors.

The oldest son was Oran Arms Curtis who was born in Eugene, Indiana, June 2, 1829, and while quite young - at the age of twenty years - was married to Isabelle Quick; they only lived together a few years when they were divorced. There were two children born of this marriage; Harvey and John Curtis.

After Oran Curtis was divorced from his first wife, he joined a wagon circus and after remaining with it a season he went out into the territory of Kansas and arrived in Topeka in the year 1856 and was for a time employed by the Pappans to assist in running or operating a ferry boat across the Kansas River. Later in that year, he went up into Iowa, but returned to Kansas in 1858 and again was employed on the ferry by Louis Pappan and early in the year 1859 he was married to Helene Pappan, the oldest daughter of Louis and Julie Pappan. There were two children born as the result of this marriage - Charles and Elizabeth Curtis.

Article No. II

At the time of my birth, January 25, 1860, my parents were living in a log house, which was located near the landing of the Pappan Ferry on the north bank of the Kansas River. My sister, Elizabeth, was born September 2, 1861. When the great Civil War came, my father, like thousands of others, volunteered in the Union Army and soon after his enlistment, he was sent to the front. When the 15th Kansas Cavalry was organized my father was commissioned Captain of Company F of the Regiment. Mother, sister and I were left behind.

Mother died in 1863 of what was then known as the black fever. We two children were taken to the home of our grandparents, William and Permelia Curtis, who then lived on a farm near the old town of Mount Florence. In addition to running a farm my grandparents kept a stopping place for the travelers and ran the stage barn where the stage horses and mules and the horses carrying the pony express were exchanged. Their house was very large for the times in that section of the country; the barn and feedlot would accommodate a large number of horses and mules.

The days at the farm were exciting and many of the events are indelibly written upon my mind. I can remember the old stage coaches and the reckless and fearless drivers, the couriers on horseback, the long line of freight wagons drawn by oxen, mules and horses, the old prairie schooners and the wild western characters that were then so well known in that part of the country; the many soldiers and the dances that were given in their honor in the large dining room; the great corn crib full of corn; the cattle; the horses; the chickens and guinea hens; the hog killing in the fall; the great piles of apples, potatoes, turnips and cabbage that were covered with straw and dirt to keep for winter use; the rendering of the lard, the making of soap and candles, the boiling of hominy, the making of rag carpets and the quilting bees, the knitting of all kinds of comforts for the folks at home and the soldiers in the field; the taking of the wheat and corn to mill and bringing back our own flour and corn meal.

The nearest mill was several miles away in Ozawkie. We drove over in the morning and back in the afternoon. The Grasshopper River near the dam was a great place for fish and the channel cats were plentiful, so sometimes we would stay all night and do a little fishing. Youngster as I was, I can still remember the trips and the great joy it brought me when I was allowed to go along.

The first school I attended was in the old log school house, with its wooden benches and its old fireplace. It was located about two miles west of my grandfather's farm and was known as the Seals School. Why I was allowed to go is not known to me. I was too young to study and so I judge I was sent so that the folks at home would know I was out of trouble.

In 1864 or 1865, my grandfather Curtis purchased a large part of Kaw Mile Four from my grandmother, Julie Gonvil Pappan. This land covered what is now known as North Topeka, Kansas. Grandfather Curtis laid out the town of Eugene, and he did it on a big scale. He gave a strip of land, 400 feet wide by 1600 feet long, to the Union Pacific Railway for railroad purposes. He set aside 150 feet by 170 feet for a public school, and he gave a lot 75 feet by 175 feet to each of the three churches, Methodist, Congregational and Baptist. He erected a large hotel just south of the Union Pacific Depot and built a livery stable with feedlots just a block west of the hotel. He put up buildings for a post office and general store.

There was a good reason for his making such liberal provisions for schools, churches and the railroad. Topeka had no railroad, the Union Pacific desired to build on the north side of the river and the old and historic town of Indianola was a thriving border village nestling in a bend of the Big Soldier Creek, about three miles northwest of Topeka. It was a trading center for the Potawatomi Indians; had a fine large hotel, general store, etc., and it was fighting hard for the Union Pacific Railroad. If it secured the road, its future was assured; if it lost the road, the town was

Racing: Indian Style

doomed. The railroad went to Eugene or North Topeka. A good pontoon bridge was built across the Kansas River. Eugene was made a part of the city of Topeka and has since been known as North Topeka. The Union Pacific was built into North Topeka and the first train pulled into the station January 1, 1866. Indianola began to decrease in population; houses were moved to North Topeka and in a few years the frontier town of Indianola had disappeared and was no more. The ground that was formerly covered by houses and was the center of business activity and the scene of active western life is now a field and the town of Indianola is unknown.

Eugene or North Topeka was a most interesting place and it was a typical frontier town; it had a main street that ran east and west and was known as Railroad Street; the buildings erected on it faced the depot and railroad right-of-way. The Curtis house, the Parks House, the Antietam and other saloons and their accompanying gambling rooms, the post office, the livery stable, the general store and other establishments were all located on this street. The games of chance that were common in those days, such as poker, faro, montee, chuckoluck, etc., were going in full blast.

The genuine characters of the plains and frontier were daily seen on the street and in the various places of entertainment. Once in a while Wild Bill would come down from the western part of the state; he always attracted a great deal of attention; he was tall and as straight as an Indian, his hair was long and black and his eyes were of the piercing kind, he was a great gambler and a dead shot. When he visited North Topeka the men and boys would follow him from place to place and he seemed to like the attention he attracted.

Then there was Abram Burnett, a half breed Potawatomi Indian, but who claimed to be a full blood; he was no doubt the broadest and heaviest man who ever lived in the state, he was so large that when he rode in a lumber wagon there was no room on the seat for any other person, not even a little boy. He was educated in the schools of Indiana and Michigan. His home was on a beautiful mound a few miles southwest of Topeka. When he died, he was buried in his Indian allotment and since his death the piece of elevated ground has been and is still called Burnett's Mound. He was good natured and always full of fun and greatly enjoyed. The attention he attracted - the illustration below will give you some idea of his size. It is said that he weighed 450 pounds.

Charles Curtis

    In those first days in the life of Eugene, one could see almost any day such prominent characters as Kaw Charles, Joe Jim, a Potawatomi, Kaw and Osage interpreter, Louis Ogee and George Young, leading members of the Citizen Band of Potawatomi Indians. There was one man who will be long remembered, that was old Dr. McClease. This kindly old man made regular visits to North Topeka,

Racing: Indian Style

he was known as the saddle bag doctor and was loved by the people in every house in that section of the country. I can remember him as he would ride into town, he had a full long white beard, his hair was gray, his medicine bag hung on each side of the back of the saddle and the contents were mostly quinine and calomel, and he frequently resorted to bleeding. I could name others but space and time will not permit.

In the winter months the Buffalo hunters would come in with their great wagons of frozen buffalo meat, they found a ready market for their products and a wagon load would usually be sold in a short time. The last wagon load I remember of having been brought into North Topeka was in the winter of 1873 and 1874. I recall this load well because the owner gave me a very large piece of the choice cut for piloting him around to the houses where I thought he would most likely find a ready market.

I lived at the Curtis house with my grandparents, William and Permelia Curtis, until the fall of 1866. The first school I attended in North Topeka or Eugene was held in the old log house in which I was born; then there was a school in the second story of a frame house which had been erected on Jackson Street, just off the old Union Pacific Depot.

In 1866, I went to live with my grandparents Louis and Julie Pappan. They resided on the Kaw or Kansas Indian Reservation in Morris County, Kansas. I attended the Quaker Mission School which was maintained at the agency.

My experience among the Indians will never be forgotten. I could talk the Kaw language and was able to talk and understand French. I visited the lodges, wigwams, teepees, and the Indian villages, watched the dances, attended the council meetings, and was always on hand at the feasts. One of the most interesting events was the Government cattle issue. I attended but two - they were very exciting. The Texas steers with their great longhorns were placed in what was known as the issue pen, those that were to be killed at the time were turned out and as each steer passed through the gate a number of bucks or young Indians on their ponies would start after it and it would only be a few minutes until it was down, killed, skinned and ready for the knife. After the required number were killed, the others were kept in the pen and fed for a few days and they were then turned out for use in the future.

Charles Curtis

I can remember the squaw corn, it was very sweet and the grains were highly colored. We raised it in great quantities and dried much of it in the summer and fall for winter use. I helped jerk the buffalo meat the members of the tribe would bring in from their hunting trips. We would jerk it and place the strips across a long pole to dry.

We gathered wild grapes and would dry them by the bushel, and we also gathered hazelnuts, walnuts and hickory nuts.

I saw the full bloods bury their dead, sometimes they were placed on the side of a hill and great rock piled on them, their ponies were killed and placed on the graves. Some were buried in the ground and the relatives made all the arrangements they thought necessary in order to enable the dead to enter the Happy Hunting Ground, and their ponies, tomahawks and trinkets were buried with them. Some were placed in the branches of trees and the relatives of the dead would mourn their departed one for days and their moaning, wailing and chanting was sad indeed; it seems that even now I can hear some of the wailing that went up in the early morning from those poor people whose loved ones had been taken and they are the saddest memories in my recollection.

I do not remember when I learned to ride and swim but have been told that my mother taught me both. I know I was always fond of both and have been able to do both from my earliest recollection. I would go hunting, riding, fishing and swimming with the boys on the Reservation. I took part in all the games of the boys of my age. I had my bows and arrows, some of the arrows were pointed, some had round blunt heads and others had the small spike. I joined with the boys in shooting the arrows at nickels, dimes and quarters which visitors would place in split sticks.

I remember the grasshoppers that came in 1867. They did not do much damage but gave great annoyance.

I remained on the reservation until the Cheyenne Indians made a raid on the Kaw and Kansas Indians on the second day of June, 1868. This raid was made by several hundred well-armed and mounted Cheyenne Indian warriors. A few years ago, I was asked to write my recollection of the raid and of my trip from the agency to Topeka and the article I wrote was as follows:

Racing: Indian Style

"November 25, 1916.

My dear Mr. Steele:

 Please accept my thanks for your kind letter of recent date, inviting me to attend the meeting of the Old Settlers' Association in Shawnee County, December the 5th. I assure you nothing would give me greater pleasure than to again meet the men and women who have done so much to make of Kansas the great state that she is.

 I note what you say with reference to my writing you a letter in case I am unable to be present, relative to a trip I made from Council Grove to Topeka, "way back in '68". I doubt very much if such a story would be of interest to the men and women now living, who blazed their way to the frontier in the early days. They did their share in the fight which made Kansas free, enduring hardships which only true pioneers understand, and with them Indian raids, and tales of battles between Indian tribes are not so soon forgotten.

 In 1868, I was attending the Indian Mission School on the Kansas Indian Reservation in Morris County. I lived with my grandparents on my mother's side, Louis and Julie Pappan, my grandmother being a member of the tribe.

 One day about noon in the summer of '68, a few boys, of whom I was one, were playing on the bank of the creek when we heard a number of Indians singing war songs. We ran to the road to ascertain the cause and were surprised to find numerous members of the Kaw tribe, their faces and bodies covered with war paint, bear claws around their necks, riding their ponies in single file and equipped with bows, arrows, and other weapons. I asked one of the warriors at the head of the line what the trouble was and he told me the Cheyenne were coming to fight the Kaw and they were going to meet them. He said the members of the tribe at the main Indian village and further down the creek had been notified and asked us to go up the creek and inform those who lived on their separate allotments.

 The Indians then rode on and we proceeded to notify my grandparents and others of the coming of the Cheyenne and the consequent danger.

 It was not long after that that we were given orders to go up to the

Charles Curtis

Mission, or trading post, and the older men, women and children were gathered into an old unused barn. They had with them their bows and arrows, shotguns, rifles and old muskets. Shortly after the Kaw and Cheyenne appeared near the village the war parties were fighting in circles, in Indian fashion. I remember some of the older men in our place of refuge shot through the holes and cracks in the walls.

Shortly after this the Cheyenne began a retreat and soon left the scene of battle. At the time I did not know the cause of their sudden departure, but after we left the building I discovered quite a number of people had come down from Council Grove, and I judged the men had frightened them away.

All at the agency had expected that the Cheyenne were on one of their raids and feared the number who attacked the Kaw were only a small band of those out on a similar errand. It was expected that there would be another and more serious attack, and our people were anxious as they did not know how far the Cheyenne raiders might actually go. It was thought best that someone should hasten to Topeka and notify those along the way that the Cheyenne were coming.

I volunteered to make the trip. When we heard the Cheyenne were coming, the horses and ponies were driven to pasture, some distance from my grandparents' home, so there was no horse or pony for me to ride. I, therefore, started out on foot, traveling during the night as rapidly as I could and notifying the campers whom I passed on the way and what few settlers there were (there being but few, and those on the creek) about the coming of the Cheyenne.

I arrived in Topeka, I think about noon of the next day. I told the story to my father and grandfather, and remember they went over to the State House and by night we had word that the Cheyenne were not coming on but were returning to their reservation.

It was a very exciting time for the others as well as for me, but being accustomed to frontier life, I did not mind the trip. I had been over the road many times and even had I not known it, I could not have missed it as it was the main highway (a part of the way it was the old Santa Fe trail) and well-marked by camping places, the remains of broken down wagons and the bones of horses and oxen which had died as a result of the hard journeys they had been forced to make over the plains.

I did not, until a few years ago, know that any note had been

Racing: Indian Style

made of this incident, and was surprised when I read an article, written by Mr. Huffaker, describing the raid of the Cheyenne and also mentioning the little part I played in that event. I understand this paper has been reproduced by Mr. George P. Morehouse in his History of the Kaw Indians. *The above is a brief statement of my recollection of the raid and trip and I hope it may prove of some interest to the Old Settlers of Shawnee County. We, the sons and daughters of the pioneers are proud of the work of our fathers and mothers. They came to Kansas to help free it and to reclaim what was known, when they came west, as a desert. They have transformed the plains into the garden spot of the world and have, in Kansas, created one of the greatest states of the Union."*

After the Cheyenne raid my folks at Topeka would not let me return to the Kaw Reservation, and I lived with my father and step-mother (father having in the meantime married Lucy Jay of Olathe, Kansas).

I attended school for the remaining days of the school term and later in the summer went to live with my grandparents, William and Permelia Curtis. They owned and ran The Curtis House and William Curtis owned a grocery store and kept in connection with the hotel a livery and feed barn. He owned a couple of running horses, Brown Tom and Flatfoot. Tom was a very fine-looking horse and a good fast racer. Flatfoot was well named, for his hoofs were broad and flat. He was quite fast but very unreliable. This was largely due to the fact that he was blind in one eye and had been abused and was very nervous and excitable. These horses were frequently matched to run against other horses that were owned in and around Topeka and those that were being taken through by traveling race horse men. Grandfather had no light weight rider and for this reason was frequently caught at a disadvantage because of the weight his horses carried. The races were usually for short distances - from three hundred to eight hundred yards and with catch weight.

While on the Reservation I had ridden all kinds of Indian ponies and had ridden in a number of pony races and was considered a good and fearless rider, and soon after I went to live with my grandparents, I was put to riding the running horses.

In the fall of 1868, I rode my first real horse race. Flatfoot was matched to run against a very fast horse that had just been brought into the locality. The race was a quarter of a mile on a straight track and I rode Flatfoot. It was a regular frontier crowd that gathered to see the race; the betting was not very lively because of the rumors of the speed of the strange horse. The starter and judges were soon selected; we riders were lifted to our mounts - we both rode bareback, and the horses were soon ready for the word "go".

Old Hinshaw and Tip, two local race horse men, were looking after Flatfoot at the start. The starter soon gave the word and both horses were off. Flatfoot took the lead and held it until the crowd at the lower end of the track was reached. The shouts for the local horse were loud and long but were too much for him and he broke from the track and before I could get him back the other horse was in the lead and won by a neck. This race settled Flatfoot and he was put in the livery and he made a good livery horse but the race was not the last for me; it was but the beginning of a riding career, which lasted until 1876, and the next year I became a full-fledged jockey.

In 1869, William Curtis heard of a roan mare, Carrie, owned in southern Kansas and was reported to be the fastest eight-hundred-yard horse in the west; she was owned by a man who had moved into Kansas from Missouri and he wanted to farm and was anxious to sell or trade his race horse. Grandfather Curtis took a trip to the farm of the owner and found the mare was out in the pasture. She was brought in, was very fat and in no condition to be given a tryout, but the owner, anxious to get rid of her, was very loud in her praise and said he was willing to give her a tryout with Brown Tom and named the price he was willing to take for her.

Eight hundred yards were stepped off in the road and the trial was given. The little mare left Tom from the start and demonstrated she could run. She was purchased and Brown Tom and Carrie became a racing pair that were destined to travel many miles together and became quite noted for their speed. They were first put into training at the Curtis barn in North Topeka and Carrie was soon molded into shape and it was not long before a match race was arranged between her and a local horse called Tinker owned by Phil Gilman. This race was eight hundred yards and was on a straight track on the land upon which that part of the city of Topeka now known as Potwin is located.

Racing: Indian Style

The crowd was large and betting was spirited. Tinker was well known and had won a good many races. Carrie was unknown. I ride Carrie and Tom Carr, a local rider, rode Tinker. Phil Gilman was at Tinker's head and turned him, while I handled my mount without assistance. There was some little jockeying at the start but soon the word "go" was given and the horses were off. They were neck and neck for a few hundred yards when Carrie began to run away from her opponent. She won easily by some forty or fifty feet.

Carrie had shown her speed and from then on, no owner of a local horse would take a chance. In the fall of 1870, William Curtis concluded to take his two runners to western Kansas. At that time, Ellsworth was the cattle town of that part of Kansas. It was the gathering place of the owners of the Texas LongHorn Cattle; with every herd there was usually one or more running ponies or horses. We had a wagon fitted up for the use of the men who went along and I rode one of the runners and led the other.

On the way up, I remember one night we camped on the east side of the Fort Riley Military Reservation; there was a running stream that came down out of the hills which were to the north, and the water was as soft as rain water. We not only took advantage of the nice soft water for ourselves but we gave the runners a good washing and rub down.

The next day we passed the old stone building, the first Territorial Capitol of Kansas. I little dreamed then that in forty years from then I would be in the Congress of the United States and among other things asking that the old building be put in repair; that the banks of the Smoky River be ripraped so as to prevent the building from tumbling into the river and that the building be turned over to the state, but that is what did happen in 1901.

Article No. III

We went on west past Junction City. I remember well the wild plums in the sand hills at the side of the road, and the bubbling spring on the north bank of the river. We all went down to the river bank and looked at the sand and water boil up and it was interesting to look at - it was called the bubbling, boiling or sand spring. Many years after I was told that the bubbling and peculiar movement of the sand was caused by gas.

We went on west and then next thing of interest to me, as a boy, was the great prairie dog town just west of Solomon. I have seen many prairie dog towns but this was the largest I had ever seen. I remember the tales they told about the prairie dogs and their neighbors and tenants, the rattlesnakes, the owls and other living things. I thought then they were told me to keep me near the camp but I have since learned that they were not exaggerated.

We passed through the old Fort *(Harker)* and camped in a clump of trees by the historic spring that breaks through the rocks which line the well-known draw, at the head of which is a great soft rock. We went up to this rock and read the names of the Buffalo hunters, pioneers and cattlemen which had been cut in the rock. There were many who were well known then but have long since been forgotten. We stayed a day or two at the spring to give our horses a chance to rest up and to give the men a chance to visit Ellsworth and select a good camping place near the town.

We got well acquainted with the suttler at the fort. He was a sporting man and as he said, "loved to see the ponies run" and he gave

Charles Curtis

us lots of information in regard to the men and horses the cattlemen had with their outfits.

Ellsworth is in the valley of the Smoky; was then the main town on the Texas Cattle trail - it was the meeting place for the buyers from every section of the country and a stopping place for the outfits with their long horns from Texas on the way to the Indian reservations in the northwest. The men usually spent a few days at Ellsworth and it was a typical frontier cattle town. There were business houses, great general stores, dance halls, gambling places and saloons. Every gambling house ran several monte layouts because this was the game for the men from Texas - there were ferro, chuckoluck and poker tables. In the dance halls there were to be seen women of every grade and condition from fresh young girls just starting out to those who had been in the game for years and followed the trail, and then there were the experienced madames who ran the places and knew the business from A to Z.

I shall never forget Ellsworth as I saw it then. The old red-light district which passed with the change in the run of the trail. No one would think of the quiet law-abiding Ellsworth of today as the noisy cattle town of 1869 and 70.

The men found a camping place down by the river and it was not long before there was an 800 yard race matched between Carrie and a Texas horse, which had met all the horses on the trail and had not lost a

Racing: Indian Style

single race. He had won over the fastest horse in Ellsworth and the cow men, gamblers and members of the sporting fraternity were anxious to get their money up on him. There were a few outside our own crowd; a banker, a lawyer, the suttler of the Fort and the madam of one of the sporting houses, who backed our horse, but, my grandfather was there and he had plenty of money and took all the bets he could get.

The race was run on a straight track near the river and in the edge of the red-light district. There was a large crowd; all the inmates of the sporting houses, all the gamblers, all the cowboys and cattle owners were out. When the time came to take the horses to the starting place, there was but little delay.

The Texas horse was ridden by a young Texas cowboy who weighed about 110 pounds. I rode Carrie and weighed about 70 pounds. Neither of us had saddles. The horses were soon given the word and Carrie led from the start and won the race by three or four lengths. If I had been a rider of experience, I would have won by a length but I was afraid to take a chance and made my mount do her best.

I never knew how much money our crowd won but I know it was a large sum and the gamblers and the madam insisted on taking me to her house and then up town and bought me a new suit of clothes, boots, hat and all and the madam had a new jockey suit made for me. I was proud of my good luck; the suit was a good one. They gave me money and bought me candy and presents and they came to our camp every day.

We could get no more races and soon left. I was anxious to stay. I had never been so petted in my life and I liked it.

We went from there west intending to go to Fort Hays but some of the men wanted to go on a buffalo hunt and they left the race horses in camp with the trainers and the rider and so I was cheated out of a wild time.

We soon returned to Topeka and went from there to Lawrence, when I rode Lop-eared John a half mile on the old figure eight track and from there we went to Kansas City. In 1871, we went to a few county fairs in Kansas and St. Mary's, Kansas, at the time of the last big payment to the Citizens

Band of Potawatomi Indians. The payment was made in the old store house near the college - the old house still stands.

There was to be over $ 150,000.00 paid out and the Indians, traders, gamblers, horse men and spectators were there in great numbers. I will never forget my first night in St. Mary's. We arranged to keep our horses in a private barn. We slept in the barn but took our meals at the hotel. I have heard the soldiers of the world war tell of the "cooties" but I doubt if they could beat those of St. Mary's.

I went into the old hotel for supper, the office room was crowded. The street in front was jammed. I washed for supper and went to the comb case, which was a tin comb holder, which was fastened under the regulation small hotel mirror, and I thought I saw the big comb moving. I took hold of one end and lifted it out and it was just a mass of big crawling cooties. I dropped the comb, fixed my hair with my fingers.

We had one race at St. Mary's. There was so much waged on the other horse and well-known Carrie won, as was her habit.

That fall, we again went to the Kansas County Fairs. The spring of 1872 found our horses in good shape and running faster than ever before, we had a number of racers, went to a number of fairs winding up at  Kansas City. There were all kinds of horses at Kansas City - runners and trotters, short and long distances, but, I remember the great attraction was the then great horse Ethan Allen, who was to trot, as I remember it, against a runner or a running mate. He was to start about three o'clock and there was a great crowd to see him. I was permitted to remain at the track long enough to see him and then I was to take Tom over towards the gate to exercise him.

The crowd was large, we could not get along over regular training ground outside the track. As I neared the gate, I heard a great commotion, the crowd was excited. As I got near I was advised that robbers had ridden up and taken the gate receipts of the day. I hastened back to our stalls and our horses got no more exercise that day. I was afterwards told that the James Boys had done the job and had gotten away with about ten thousand dollars.

Racing: Indian Style

At this fair, I really got my first experience as a rider and for the first time realized the danger to which every jockey is liable. Our horses only ran short distances - 800 yards and a half mile. They were not entered in any of the regular races - we depended upon making match races so I was free to ride in any of the regular races when my services were wanted. My first mount was a small bay horse that was hard to handle and ride and was a known bolter. I succeeded in keeping him on the track but did not get a place in the race but the fact that I was able to manage him brought me a mount the next day on a horse called Bob. He was a bad actor and had a habit of putting both front feet into the ground just as the crowd began to shout for the leading horse and his rider usually went over his head and Bob would lose the race and his owners and backers who knew him to be one of the fastest short distance horses in the country usually lost their money.

I was advised of his trick and agreed to ride him. The trainer advised me and so did the rider that he had a habit of throwing one ear back as the crowd began to yell, then jump stiff and the race was over.

I bought two new steel spurs and a well wrapped rawhide. I was given the side next to the fence and when the race was called there was a big crowd gathered at the end of the track, both horses were well known and both were fast. We were not long in getting the word. Bob was leading and when we were about fifty yards from the end the crowd began to yell. I saw Bob's ear come back and the next second I socked both spurs into his sides with all the force I possessed and at the same time hit him on the flank with the whip - he sprang forward with a mighty jump and won the race by a good length.

The success in the race brought a request that I ride the outlaw, Headlight in a race the next day. Headlight was a fine-looking animal and had great speed but he was dangerous, hard to manage and usually went over the fence at the first turn. I was assured if I could get him around the first turn there would be no trouble and so I undertook the job of riding him. In the morning, I eased him on the first turn and he acted fine. There were eight or ten horses entered and all of them were considered fast so there were but few, if any, to bet on Headlight but he had many admirers.

We had a time starting. I kept him well in hand and turned him myself. At last we were off and as we reached halfway round the first turn he made a break for the fence and I sent a spur into his side with all the force I could muster. He went up against the high board fence and we all (fence, horse and boy) went over the embankment. My breath was knocked out, my hands were bruised and bleeding and I carry the scars today of that awful fall.

Our horses were doing so well and in all trial runs had made such good records that we concluded to take them to Independence, Kansas. Our trainer concluded he would enter Tom in some of the long races and he was entered in a number of them and won. He had never been run in a greater distance than three quarters of a mile before.

We had quite an experience at Independence with the fast 300 yard pony Billy Button - he was considered about as fast as any of the

Racing: Indian Style

horses in that section for that distance but his owner had fixed him up so no one would know him - they hoped to fool some owner of a fast horse. Billy had a bunch of gray hairs at the root of his tail, these had been made black, he had been roached and otherwise changed. I had ridden horses that were kept in stalls adjoining the one in which he was stabled at Kansas City at the last two fairs and I knew him well but when our trainer found what they were up to, he told me not to recognize the pony and after a few days bantering back and forth a match of 500 yards was made between Billy and Carrie. I felt sure Carrie could outrun him from the start but I was warned to be careful.

They day of the race was fine and a big crowd was out. A crowd had come over from Missouri and from the Indian Territory to bet on Billy and the betting was lively. That race was a greater attraction and drew a larger crowd than any other race of the week. We were not long at the post, the word "go" was given and we were off. Billy led for about 100 yards when I passed him with Carrie and won quite easily but it was a pretty race for the first 200 yards.

We had intended to close the racing season at Independence but our horses had been so successful that Grandfather Curtis was persuaded to send them south for the winter. That trip south in a covered wagon and on horseback I shall never forget, it was wonderful. It was my first winter to miss school, but I have always felt that my experience was worth more to me than my loss by missing my books.

We fitted out at Independence; bought a big wagon, fixed it up for traveling and camping, bought a fine team of work horses. With this outfit and our then running horses we started south. There were four men and me in the party. Tip Williamson, the Manager; Doc. Hindshaw, the trainer; Bill Dawson, the cook; and Mike McCarty, the assistant trainer and owner of one of the runners.

Our first stop was Baxter Springs, Kansas. Baxter was the marketplace and trading center for the part of the Indian Territory south of it. It was full of cattle men, Indian traders and the usual crowd of sports that can be found in thriving border towns. We camped near the historic spring and remained in the town a number of days but the reputation of our horses had preceded us and we could get no matches there and so we started south into the Indian Territory. We went through Miami, in the Quapaw country, and then down through the Cherokee Reservation to

Charles Curtis

Fort Smith, Arkansas.

Soon after leaving the town of Miami, we passed a half breed and asked him about the road to Fort Smith and he was very particular in directing us but along about night we drove up to a log cabin and upon asking the old Indian about the way, he informed us by signs and other ways that we were off the road about fifteen miles and directed us the way to reach the main road and showed us a good camping place and just as he left us he said, "Watchum horses bad men take um."

We had expected to have trouble with horse thieves and had purchased locks and chains for the horses and every night three of them were locked to the wagon and the two work horses were locked to trees. About three o'clock the next morning there was an attempt to steal the horses but the locks and chains saved them. And a well-directed shot drove the thieves away. We were at the foot of the Boston mountains.

I shall never forget the trip back to the main road. We crossed one clear mountain stream thirty odd times in the few miles. When we reached the Arkansas River opposite Fort Smith, we found the river full of mush ice. The ferry boat was not running so we camped in the timber at the edge of a cane break. We could not get to town so we spent the time exploring the cane break. We found no end of rabbits, squirrels, quails and prairie chickens, wild hogs and wild turkeys and we spent two or three days hunting. One day we had a fine roasted wild pig for dinner and it was mighty fine.

When we were able to cross the river, we went over to Fort Smith but were unable to get a race so we went on south. The first night out from Fort Smith another attempt was made to steal our horses. The lock and chains again saved them and a shot from a reliable revolver drove the intruders away.

As we traveled through the territory, we found a wild country and here and there an Indian settlement. Every day or two we would pass a race track, a straight one for short races. We would always stop but the people had but little money. When a match was made it was usually for a small amount and always one-sided, for our horses were kept in good condition and after a day's rest they were ready for a race.

We found plenty of wild game, prairie chickens, wild turkey, deer and antelope. One night we camped by the side of a beautiful mountain stream in the Boston mountains. There was plenty of timber and lots of

Racing: Indian Style

game, so we were in no hurry about breaking camp in the morning, and it happened that I started out ahead riding one horse and leading the other. I had gone scarcely a mile when I saw through the trees one of the finest looking animals that I had ever seen. It was a large buck with big antlers. It was standing under the trees not far from the road. I wanted the men to get him for his antlers if for nothing else, so I turned the horses around and went back to the wagon and told the men about the buck.

Greasy Bill, the cook, took the rifle and we all went back to the place and the buck was still there. Bill raised his rifle and took aim but we heard no report from the gun; after a few seconds (which seemed minutes to us) the buck turned and disappeared among the trees. Bill threw his rifle to the ground, jumped on it with both feet and declared he had heard of hunters having a buck fit or fever but that was his first experience. From then on, he was known as, and called by the members of the party Buck.

We were told that the stores would trade goods and merchandise for deer meat, deer skins and wild turkey, so we usually managed to have something to trade at every little town that we passed through. We went to Fort Gibson. I shall always remember my surprise while crossing the Arkansas river on a ferry boat. We crossed just below the place where Spring River was very noticeable and it looked for some distance as though the clear water of that river was to displace the muddy waters of the Arkansas but soon we found that muddy waters began spreading from one bank to the other and all trace of the clear water had disappeared.

We went south through McAlester. We camped one night on the banks of a small stream south of a small town and I thought it was the most beautiful place I had ever seen. We were in the timber at the foot of the mountains - it was the most beautiful view I had ever seen.

We had quite an experience at an old toll bridge. It was in bad condition. We were afraid to take our horses across and so told the bridge keeper. He told us there was a good ford five miles up the river so we started for the ford. When we arrived we found that the informant had taken a near cut on horse back and when we arrived at the ford we were informed that he held a license for ten miles up and down the river and we must pay for crossing which we did. A little way from the ford we found a beautiful spot for camping, it was near an Indian cabin, where we purchased butter and eggs and feed for the horses; corn blades, oats in the sheaf, etc.

The surroundings were wonderful, the night was fine, we built a great log fire and in the night the whippoorwills gave out their songs, the call of the whippoorwill made you want to look at the stars and think of home. We felt repaid for the extra drive and did not feel badly over the hold-up.

The next day we started for Stringtown, intending to go but a short distance each day as we had heard there were running horses over near there and we hoped to get a race. The day before we arrived in Stringtown, we had seen no prairie chickens until about camping time when we came to a small valley through which a small stream ran and here and there were small fields of corn still in the shock. As we entered the valley we saw more prairie chickens than we had seen on the entire trip. They were as thick as they could be. It was not necessary to aim at

Racing: Indian Style

any one chicken for they were flying up from the ground in every direction. In a few shots we had killed about fifteen which was all we wanted. We drove on a mile or so and went into camp. The men of the party were all pioneers of the west and it was the judgement of every one that they had never seen so many prairie chickens at one time as they saw passing through that valley in the Indian Territory.

The roads were rough and bad, the horses were showing the effects of the long trip. We came to a blacksmith shop and we had the horses shod. The blacksmith knew all about the runners whose owners lived near Stringtown and he told us we would have no trouble in making a match. We had not gone far after leaving his shop, until we noticed that Tom was a little lame. Upon examination, we found that the blacksmith had pricked him by driving the nail too high. We camped at the first good place we came to, removed Tom's shoe and doctored his foot as best we could.

The next day we concluded to make the short drive and camp a mile or two outside Stringtown, this we did. Tom was still a little lame and we felt he was in such shape that it would not be safe to run him.   Our men soon found the owner of the horse which was the favorite in the neighborhood. They also found the blacksmith had come to town. The owners of the local horses were willing to match his horse against Tom but our crowd would not do it unless the race was put off for a week. This caused the local owners to brag and blow about what his horse could do and at last we made a match between Carrie and his horse for 800 yards. Carrie won easily and our crowd was happy. We went back to camp. Here we had our first misfortune. Our fifth horse, a beautiful sorrel owned by Mike, was taken sick and died two days later and we buried him among the trees on the hill side and covered the grave with a stone. We went on to Texarkana, Sherman and then to McKinney. We had heard there

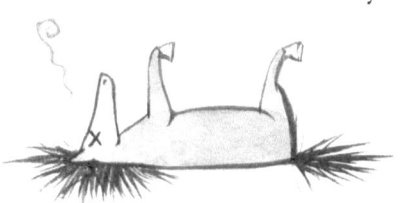

was a good half mile track there and that the town afforded a number of fast horses. Soon after arriving in Texas we saw our first grist mill run by ox power. I watched the oxen as they treaded hour after hour and never getting ahead. I felt sorry for the poor animals.

At Waco, we camped under large live oak trees; these trees extended several hundred feet back from the bank of the Brazos River, and made a fine camping place. The first thing that attracted my attention was the suspension bridge and boy-like I could not understand how it could hold up under the loads that were constantly going over it. I was so afraid of it that the first day I was to go over it into the main part of the city, I crossed the river at the ford, but after the first day, I used the bridge.

At Waco, I found for the first time in my young life that oranges were so plentiful in some places that they were given away to customers at the stores. I went into one of the largest grocery stores to buy what we needed at the camp. After completing the purchases and while waiting for the groceries to be wrapped, I noticed a large barrel of oranges and suppose my wistful look was noticed by one of the clerks, and he told me to help myself. I took one and the clerk said, "Fill your pockets, they are free to our customers." I need not add that I did as

Racing: Indian Style

I was told and that during our stay in Waco that store got all our trade.

There was a large tree on the side of the bank near our camp and I noticed that many birds would fly to a certain limb and then disappear for a few seconds and then reappear again, and so I concluded to investigate. I found a small hollow in the body of the tree and upon running my hand down into the small opening, I discovered that it was partly filled with water. For a few days after that I would hide behind a tree and when the birds would disappear in the hole in the tree, I would climb up, place my hand over the opening and catch the birds. After playing with them for awhile, I would turn them loose. Everything went nicely for a day or two, and I was having lots of fun but on the second day I noticed a beautiful red bird enter the opening. He was a wonderfully fine-looking bird and I made up my mind I would catch him and the next day after watching for some time, I saw him near the old tree and I slipped around behind it and soon the red bird lit in the tree and it was not long until he disappeared in the hole. I climbed up where I could place one hand over the hole and put the other down it for the bird. I caught it but I had no sooner tightened my hand over him until he caught my little finger between his bills and I never imagined a bird could pinch so hard; the pain was great and in a second, I turned him loose and my lesson was learned. I caught no more birds.

While at Waco a severe storm, known there as a northern, came up, the wind was high and it became quite cold. The weather was so bad and the storm so fierce that we abandoned our camp and took our horses to a livery barn and went to a hotel until the storm was over. It ended with quite a snow storm and with the snow came snow ornice birds by the thousands.

It was quite a lot of fun for me to see the merchants fix their snow bird traps. The trap consisted of a large board, held up at one end by a stick to which was attached a string that ran back to the store. I think there was a bird trap in front of nearly every store. The storekeeper or one of the clerks would sprinkle rice under the board and when the little birds gathered beneath the board, the string would be pulled, the board would fall and a lot of birds would be killed or wounded. The next day many of the hotels and restaurants had notices that bird pie would be served for dinner.

We were unable to get any races at Waco and were advised to go to San Antonio. The trip was planned to take us through a number of small towns where there were runners, across the plains and into the cattle country. We got everything in good shape for traveling and set out on the long trip. Nothing happened worthy of note until we arrived at a little town near the edge of the staked plain; here we got all information about the distances across, the amount of water needed and etc. We gave our horses a good rest and then one afternoon loaded up our wagon, filled our water barrels and bottles and started bright and early the next morning.

We needed no map to keep us on the trail for soon after we struck it, there was no missing it because it was lined with parts of broken wagons and the bones of animals that had died on that dry barren trail. We had been on the road but a short time until we began to feel the heat, and we all, men and horses, seemed to get thirsty at the same time. About noon we stopped out on the plains, no trees in sight, but we thought it a good plan to let the horses have some feed and water while we were partaking of our cold lunch. About night we could see off to the left some trees but we did not go toward them but about dusk we could see a large number of wagons near together and we knew we were near our first stopping place. When we drove up we were surprised to find a sheet of water, probably twenty-five feet wide, coming out of the side of a small hill. We followed it a little way to where it had made a big washout and there we

Racing: Indian Style

found a big pool of water, the pool was deep, the water was clear and there was plenty of water for all.

That night we talked with campers who had come across from the other direction and we found it was not quite as far to the next water, but we were warned that the first creek was strongly alkali and we were advised to water our horse before entering the creek and were told we would find a good camping place with lots of good water and wood about three miles beyond the first creek. We started early in the morning and made the last lap across the plain in good time and in good condition.

We had quite a scare at our first camp after crossing. We had been told at the midway place that certain Indians were on the warpath and they were making for the section we would likely strike. We gathered leaves, great arms full of them, and carried them to the wagon and made beds for ourselves and the horses. There was plenty of timber and we gathered great piles of wood and built a fire by the side of a large dry log. We were having a great time when we were disturbed by a peculiar noise, we thought sure it was Indians and we began to plan as to what was the best to do. We changed the position of the wagon and fixed the horses in a better position for protection and got our guns and six shooters and saw that all were fully loaded. After we had fully prepared ourselves to meet what might come, one of the men suggested that if they were Indians that as I was part Indian they would send me out to fix it up with them, but later one of the men concluded he would do a little investigating and after a few minutes he returned laughing and told us that the noise came from prairie wolves or coyotes. This caused us to build a big fire and it was not long until there was a circle of coyotes around us but they did not venture very near but they did sit on their haunches and make a lot of noise. One of the men took a few shots at them, and after a little time they disappeared. We did not know but they would return in larger numbers so two men stood guard all night and they kept a big fire going. The coyotes did not come back.

Article No. IV

After leaving our camp we came to a ranch house and during the day we passed quite a number of ranches. At one place we camped, the owner told us there was to be a large gathering of cattlemen early the next week and suggested that we better make it as there would be all kinds of sports going on there. He said he was going and the men were to arrange about driving their herds to the north. We followed his advice and started for the place of the meeting. The roads were bad and rough and we took our time. When we arrived at the place we found several hundred men camped and the first thing that attracted my attention were the men throwing twenty-dollar gold pieces at little holes in the ground. The men stood from twenty to thirty feet away and the man whose gold piece came nearest the hole got all the money. Then there were Monte, faro, chuckoluck and other gambling games going on. We had not been on the ground long until we were informed that we could get a race, and the match could likely be made the next day.

On the following morning we drove over to where the running horse was kept, as we desired to see him and look over the track. We found a fine-looking horse and he was in good condition. There were two straight tracks about twenty feet apart and about a half mile long, but there was a chute at the starting end of one of the tracks. It was well and strongly built. The floor was covered with straw and dust and had an elevation of about eight feet and it was perhaps fifty yards down to the end of the chute.

Charles Curtis

A forfeit of $50.00 a side was put up to bind both parties to a running race between our roan mare Carrie and the local horse. The distance was to be 800 yards and the race set for the next Saturday. There was great interest shown and a large crowd came from every section. On Friday night the trainer announced that he would stand guard that night; while this was a little strange, yet nothing was thought of it at that time the suggestion was made. The men were all anxious to be relieved from standing guard. The next morning when I went to the barn to give the mare a little exercise, I noticed she stood with her head down and that she was slobbering at the mouth and did not seem to be feeling well. I called the trainer's attention to her condition but he said she was all right for me to go ahead and give her the morning exercise. I saddled her and rode up to the camp and called Tip's attention to her condition and he at once announced that she had been doped and ordered that she be taken back to the stable. He worked with her until about noon and then informed the other party that he would forfeit the $50.00, or if they would postpone the race for ten days he would double the forfeit or the bet, or that he was willing to substitute Tom and give them fifty feet, or he would start Tom from a stand still at the end of the chute.

Nothing was done but the people clamored for a race and at last all bets were declared off and the horses were to run for the forfeit. The word "go" was given. Carrie was so sick she did not seem to realize a race was on, but when the other horse ran out of the chute, she seemed to gather herself and did the best she could but the other horse won. I thought if both horses had started on the ground where they could see each other that Carrie could have won, notwithstanding the fact that she had been doped.

Hinshaw, the trainer, was discharged and on the next day he began work for the owner of the other horse, and there was no doubt in the minds of any of those who saw the race but that he had doped Carrie. This was the first and only race lost by our horses on the entire trip.

This meeting brought us in contact with a cattleman who was a character, and a man who had been taken in a number of times and he was anxious to get even and when he found how fast our horses were he told us of a crowd in a town about 100 miles away that had double crossed him and our men made plans to give him a chance to get even.

We were to take our horse to Gainesville and let Carrie fully

Racing: Indian Style

recover and rest up and then we were to go to his ranch and give her a runout with a horse he had so he would know what chances we had of outrunning the horse owned by the crowd he desired to beat. We thought we might get a match in Gainesville but as we turned from a side street into the main street of the town we passed a restaurant on the corner and a man stuck his head out of a window and shouted, "Hello Charley, when did you leave Topeka?", and in a minute he was in the street shaking hands with us and before morning the town knew all about us and how fast the horses were and we got no races there.

We remained in Gainesville until Carrie had fully recovered and then we proceeded to the house of the ranchman. He told us the men he was after would not put up their money unless they thought they had a sure thing so it was arranged that I should pack my saddle and belongings and walk into the town, go to the livery barn owned by the men who had the race horse and tell them I was a race rider out of a job and if possible, I would like to get work around the barn and offer to show them what I could do as a rider.

I went into the town and to the livery barn as directed and was permitted to stay at the barn while I could look for something to do. Their rider went off and I exercised their runner and helped take care of him for a day or two. In a few days, our crowd drove in and the big ranchman and a number of cattlemen whom he had taken into the deal also appeared in town. They came to the barn, but, of course, I did not know them.

At first, they offered to run Tom against any horse in town with the understanding that he would be ridden by Tip or Mike - each man weighing about 140 pounds, and the other horse could have up anything from a feather to a man. No match could be made, then Tip stated that if he could get a boy to ride his pony he would run the little roam mare (this was Carrie) against any horse in town. The owners of the local horse began to take notice. They came to see me, to see if I would not go over and agree to ride the roam mare; that their horse could easily outrun her and that in addition to what I could get out of the strangers, they would make it all right with me.

I told them I did not care to go over to see the parties but if they came after me, I would gladly show them that I was a regular jockey and that I would ride the mare if her owners wanted me to do so.

Charles Curtis

The next day Tip and Mike came over to talk to me, wanted to size me up. They asked all manner of questions, looked at my saddle, it only weighed 1 ½ pounds. They looked at my skin tight jockey suit, asked where I had ridden and the names of some of the horses. I told them and at last they agreed to a match if I would ride for them and so the race was arranged for the next Saturday.

The ranchman was to be the stakeholder and one of the judges. One of the other cattlemen was to be the starter. The owners of the town horse managed to see me every day and I told them the horse Tom was a fast one but I didn't think the pony was very fast. It was arranged so the ranchman or one of the stockmen would hold all the stakes, but on Saturday they began to bet horses. As these were bet they were driven in a large pen or corral. A large crowd gathered, the betting was fast and quite large.

At last the hour arrived and we went to the starting place. Tip acted as turner for Carrie or pretended to. (I had always started her myself.) At last the word was given and we were off. It was easy for Carrie so I held her well in hand. I got about the middle of the distance when a dog was turned loose on my side of the straight track, and if I had not had the mare well in hand, I am satisfied she would have struck the dog and fallen; a little further on guns were discharged and I let Carrie go and she won the race by several lengths. We had arranged for Mike to be on Tom at the home end of the track. I turned quickly, raised my whip and was given the nod by the Judge and I galloped over to Mike and we lit out on the run for the home of our ranchman.

We were on the way before the town people knew what had happened. Tip and others remained in town to collect the bets. They found they had won several thousand dollars and eighteen head of horses and one mule. That night seventeen head of the horses were stolen from the pen or corral but our crowd had all the money and one horse and a mule. The ranchman was one of the happiest men I ever saw, he was perfectly satisfied, had more than evened up the old score and our crowd had several thousand dollars in winnings and the ranchman made us keep the horse and mule for good measure.

We stayed with the ranchman for several days. I will never forget the good old sorghum molasses, the hot corn-bread, the wonderful ham and other good things to eat which he supplied. We left the ranchman's home and started for Fort Worth.

Racing: Indian Style

    While at Fort Worth, Tip Williamson, who had charge of my grandfather's horse determined he would start back home and after a day or two, we had our wagon and outfit put in good order for the trip. Our first stop was at Denison, Texas. I remember our first night there - we put our horses in the livery stable, took our blankets to the hayloft and then went down to one of the big restaurants for supper and a part of us ordered Irish stew and the others beefsteak and onions. We had hot rolls, baked potatoes and coffee. It was a real supper for us all.

    The next day I had a very exciting time. Mr. Anderson, the gambler, who had joined us a few weeks before wanted to take in the gambling houses for the purpose of trying his luck and he took me with him. We entered a big gambling place, which was operated in the rear room of a saloon. The room was full of sports and there was a crowd around every table. The players were all well supplied with money, the betting was lively and large sums were changing hands at every turn of the roulette wheel, and at the drawing of every card from the Faro box. I soon got tired looking on and went out through the saloon and stood on the street by the front door.

    I had been there but a few minutes when a crowd of cowboys came riding up as fast as their ponies could run. They dismounted in front of the saloon and entered by the front door and went back into the gambling place and as they entered they began to shoot and they soon had the place cleaned out. I followed them to the door but just as I got to it a shot splintered to one side of it and I thought it time to get out and

39

this I did as fast as my little legs could carry me.

At Denison we were told that if we would visit Pine Bluffs, Arkansas, that we might get a race, so we concluded to make that town on our way back. I will never forget that trip. A part of the way there were supposed to be corduroy roads, but when we struck them, they were so bad we undertook to travel in the grass at the side of the road, but we soon found that the grass and mud would collect on the wagon wheels and so clog them that they would not turn. We bought an extra axe and two men were kept busy keeping the mud and grass out from the wheels.

After a few days of hard pulling for the teams we arrived at the point where we were to cross the Red River. The river was very high and looked dangerous, but we placed our wagon and horses on the old ferry boat and just before making a landing on the north bank of the river, the cable broke and we were carried down the river for some distance. The men on the banks were throwing ropes and doing all they could to rescue us and just as we were about to be taken under a big tree that had toppled over into the river, a rope was fastened and the ferry swung around so only one end of it went under the tree. Had the boat hit it squarely, the horses, wagon and all would have been swept in the river. It took the men some time to get the boat up the river to a place where we could unload. We were all happy when we got off the old boat.

We went to Pine Bluffs but were unable to get a race and so we started for home. Mike, whose racing pony had died and had been buried near Stringtown desired to go back by that place so he might look on the grave of his once favorite pony and as it was only a day or two out of the

Racing: Indian Style

way, we went by and camped upon the same ground that we had occupied a few months before. We all visited the grave of the pony.

On our way home, we camped one night a few miles outside of Krebs, a mining town in the Choctaw Indian country. Mike was a guard but nothing happened until about two o'clock in the morning when he saw a man coming up to the camp. He came up to the fire and acted like he was mentally unbalanced and Mike woke us all up. After we had been up for a while and all had been firing questions at our unwelcome visitor, Mike said, in a casual way, that he hadn't killed anyone for a week and he thought it was time for him to take a shot, so as to keep his hands in, and that he might as well kill the looney as not.

He had hardly spoken the words when the man started on a run from the camp. Mike fired a shot in the air and we saw no more of our man that night, but the next morning as we drove through the little town of Krebs, we saw the fellow out in front of one of the stores talking with a crowd of men. As we drove to the front of the store and stopped, our visitor of the night before disappeared. We put him down as a horse thief and I guess we were right.

Our next stop was at Fort Gibson in the Cherokee Nation. Here we met a Cherokee Freedman by the name of Tom Hall who had lived in North Topeka, Kansas, for a number of years and who had just returned to the Indian Territory. He gave us the first news from home that we had received for a long time and some of it was sad indeed. He told us of the smallpox epidemic in North Topeka in the winter and spring of 1873 and of the death of Grandfather Curtis and of Uncle Ira Curtis. We had not heard from home since early in the winter and the news of the death of these two dear and near relatives was quite a shock.

As Grandfather was the owner of the horses, we determined to push for home as fast as possible and go by the nearest route. We struck the Kansas line at Baxter Springs and Williamson and I went on the train from there to Topeka, and the others followed on with the horses. I little thought when I was traveling in the old Indian Territory, as a boy, in 1872 and 1873, that twenty-five years later, I would be in Congress drawing a measure to settle the affairs of the Members of the Five Civilized Tribes of Indians, but that is what happened, for the bill I drew, introduced and passed in the summer of 1898 was intended to protect the interest of the people of the Indian Territory.

When we arrived home in June 1873, we found that Grandfather Curtis and Uncle Ira had died in March, as had been reported to us by Tom Hall.

I cannot describe how greatly Grandfather Curtis was missed. He was a wonderful man, a real leader among men. His death seemed to change everything. I now recall how thoughtful he was of his family and those about him, his horses, cattle, hogs, chickens and pigeons. Every fall he made full preparation for the coming winter, the hog killing, always ten or twelve, the smoking and curing of the meats, the rendering of the lard, the making of the lye hominy, the moulding of the candles, the making of soft soap, the drying of the apples, peaches and wild grapes, the sweet corn, the red peppers, the mounds of potatoes, cabbages and turnips. The making of sauerkraut and sausages, the gathering of walnuts, hickory and hazel nuts, the making of apple butter, the putting up of jellies and preserves and lots of mincemeats and various kinds of pickles, the cribs of corn and stacks of hay and fodder. These wise preparations for the winter months were always made under the watchful eyes and careful direction of Grandfather and Grandmother Curtis.

I have many vivid and delightful memories of the years of my boyhood but none are more pleasant that those spent at the old home of My Grandparents, William and Permelia Curtis.

Racing: Indian Style

The estate was being settled. The horses were sold at public auction and they brought a good price. The purchaser was a farmer who had always been more or less interested in horses and it was his intention to train the horses and enter them at the various fairs in the fall. I went out as his jockey, but soon after we arrived at the farm, the sons of the new owner thought they had a right to use the runners as they pleased and so in place of going into training the horses were ridden to town every day and were given frequent "tryouts" on the public roads to and from town.

It was apparent that the horses could do nothing under the new owner and after a month or two I told him that it would be wasting time unless the horses were placed on a track and given regular training. He thought there was plenty of time and I quit my job as a jockey for him. I hated to leave the horses and did so with a sad heart. I never saw Tom after that day but did see Carrie once after that.

When I returned home, I found a letter from Colonel Jennison asking me to come to Leavenworth and ride for him. His offer was liberal but when I arrived at the track and sized up the horses, the outlook was not promising. I agreed to stay with him a month and give his horses a good tryout. They were well bred but had no speed and after a couple of weeks, I told the Colonel that his horses were not fast enough to justify him in entering them in the fall races at St. Joseph, Kansas City and other places. He agreed to give his fastest horse a real tryout on a regular track and then determine what to do.

A week at a track was enough for him and he concluded to stop training. I returned to Topeka. I had no engagements and went over to the Fair Grounds and was soon employed at one of the stables to ride Lop-Eared John, a very fast local horse. I was given permission to ride other horses that were on the track for training. The Fair came on and John was matched to run against a horse owned by Dan Lamaster of Kansas City, Missouri.

It was understood that I was to ride John but on the night before the race was to take place, a young lightweight rider was brought over from St. Joseph, Missouri, and I was told the boy was to ride Lop-Eared John. I asked why I was not allowed to ride him and was told that my Uncle Charles LaTourette was betting on the Missouri horse and that they did not care to take any chances.

They wanted me to work on but I asked for my pay, took my

saddle and belongings and started for home. As I was passing through the gate, Mrs. Mecham, with whom most of the horsemen and riders took their meals, called me in and asked the trouble and after explaining the matter to her she asked me to stay at the house for a time. It was not long until Mr. Lamaster came driving through the Fair Ground gates. Mrs. Mecham stopped him and told him all about the new rider for Lop-Eared John. Mr. Lamaster called me out to the buggy and asked me if I would ride his horse. I told him I would be glad to do so, but I did not know his horse, had never been on him and doubted if I could get the speed out of him that a rider could who was used to his ways. Mr. Lamaster said he knew me and was willing to take a chance.

I went to his stable for the night and the next afternoon was mounted on his horse that was to race against the favorite horse of my home-town, Topeka. I had told Mr. Lamaster that I knew Lop-Eared John's little faults and I would like to ride his horse in my own way - no instructions from the trainer. The permission was given.

At the proper hour the Fair Grounds were crowded, we were not long in starting. I trailed around the first turn and down the backstretch at the lower turn. I watched John and saw him swerve for the outside of the track and I knew that unless his rider was careful he would go to the extreme outside which he did. I took advantage of the situation, held my mount close against the inside fence and urged him to his fullest speed. Before my opponent knew what was up, I was more than a full length ahead of his horse and he was unable to pass me on the home stretch and I won by nearly a half a length. It was a happy day for me. I was well paid for my ride as I had won when nearly everyone thought I would lose. I had won on the slowest horse. The pay for winning was very liberal and gladly received by me as I was anxious to enter school the next week and needed books and clothing.

The next day I had an experience which came near ending disastrously for me as a rider. I was mounted on Brown Bess and there was a jockey riding in the race who had a reputation of being rough and I was warned to look out for him. Bess was very fast but a very nervous and excitable horse and when she lost her head she was bound to lose.

We started in good shape and a number of horses were running well together, as they would say on the track, neck and neck, and as we reached the lower turn I managed to get the pole and Bess was running fine but about halfway around the turn a horse came up to my side and I recognized the rider whom I was told to watch. Just as he got to my side he threw out his foot and caught Bess in the breast with his spur. I at once struck him over the hands with my whip and he dropped the bridle reins, his horse went wild to the outside of the track and Bess was throwing her head up and down. I was able to finish with the crowd and the rider whom I had hit claimed a foul.

We were taken into the Judges stand and allowed to make our statements and it looked bad for both as the Judges did not seem to believe either of us and were about to hold us both responsible when Jim Harr, who was a riding police on the inside of the track, was called to the Judges stand, and as luck would have it, he happened to be at the inside of the track at the point where the fouling occurred. He corroborated my story as to the other boy having spurred Bess in the breast before I hit him with my whip. The other boy was ruled off the track and I was warned not to defend myself while riding but to let the Judges deal with the offenders. As there were at least two horses ahead of us where the fouling occurred the Judges let their announcement, as to the result of the race, stand.

This instance resulted in a friendship between Mr. Harr and me that lasted as long as he lived and it was my pleasure, after I was elected to Congress to recommend him and secure his appointment as a postmaster in a little town where he lived and was doing business.

After the Fair, I returned to my home in North Topeka and entered school and remained in school until the close of the term in June, 1874. During the school term of 73 and 74, I sold apples at the trains at the noon hour and helped Mr. McDonald in his store Saturdays and got his books in shape Saturday nights and Sundays. Mr. McDonald could neither read nor write and kept a memo of accounts by making marks and the old man knew the name of every customer and had their accounts so that no complaints were made when the bills were presented. How he did it, no one knows, but he did.

Article No. V

    I will never forget the winter of '73 and '74. It was hard in many ways. There was one thing though which I remember with pleasure. It was in regard to the last wagon load of buffalo meat which I remember of having been brought into Topeka. In January, a man drove up to one of the wagon yards on the north side. He had a big wagon heavily loaded with frozen buffalo meat. He wanted someone to pilot him around the town, who knew the people who would most likely want the most and I was suggested. I went with him and we sold the load out before the night. He would not pay me in cash but laid aside a big piece of a hind quarter and when we had sold out all but the one piece he drove me home and carried the piece of buffalo meat in the house and gave it to me for my day's work. We took the meat outside and placed it in a safe place in the woodshed and we had buffalo meat for days.

    Early in May of '74, I was offered a contract with Cooper and Darnell to ride Sleepy Joe and Sorrel Dan. I accepted with the understanding that I was not to report until school was out in June. As soon as school closed, I reported to Louisville, Kansas, where Cooper and Darnell were keeping their horses and putting them in shape for racing in the fall, and I found it was their intention to take the horses south in the Indian Territory, Arkansas and Texas for the winter, and I agreed to stay with them until after the fall races and then would determine about the trip south.

    While training the horses at Louisville in the summer of 1874, it was my duty to exercise the horses every day. I was in Louisville when the grasshoppers came in 1874. I will never forget the day they came, nor the great destruction they did that year. On the afternoon they came, I was out exercising Sleepy Joe and was two or three miles from the stable. All at once it seemed as though a great dark cloud had come between the sun and me, and in a few seconds, grasshoppers began to light on the ground. As soon as they lit they began to eat everything in reach. The farmers tried to save their crops but they were unable to save much of anything. The grasshoppers ate everything that was green and tender. Taking the leaves of trees, the blades on the corn stalks, peaches down to the pits, newspapers, old rags and in short everything they could find.

It was not long until covered wagons could be seen coming in from the western part of the State. On the sides were all kinds of printed and written phrases and comments. Some quite funny, some sad, but all reminders of the great damage that had been done by the grasshoppers. They had eaten everything the farmers had raised, they caused many of the sturdy men and women who had been among the pioneers of our state to leave their homesteads and take what they had left and go back to their old home states so that they might earn a living for their families.

We remained in Louisville until about the first part of September, 1874, when we started for Wichita, Kansas, where there was to be one week of racing events. The night before we were to start on our trip the two gray work horses were killed by lightning but the men purchased other horses and we started our trip by wagon across the country. Everything green had been eaten up by the grasshoppers and most of the creeks were dry because of the drouth that year. We found water and were able to buy some feed from the farmers until we reached Council Grove, Kansas. We remained at the Grove for a few days and were able to make a match between Sorrel Dan and a local horse. The race was run in the public road a few miles east of the town and only a few miles from the old Kansas Indian Mission where I attended school from 1866 to 1868, but my grandparents, Louis and Julie Pappan had removed with the Kansas tribe of Indians to their new reservation in the then Indian Territory, and while I did not see any of my relatives at the race or during my stay at Council Grove, yet, I did meet many of the men and women who had been interested in the Indian Agency.

At the side of the track and just before the start I remember meeting Judge Johnson, a lawyer of Council Grove, who was about the only

Racing: Indian Style

local man betting on the horse I was riding, and he said he was doing it because he remembered how I used to ride the Indian ponies and he knew I would win if it were in the horse.

We had no trouble in selecting a starter and the judges. The local men were so overconfident that they were careless in the handling of the horse at the starting place. The word "go" was soon given and Sorrel Dan, the horse I rode, led from the start! I won the race by a good length. Our men won a lot of money on the race and it was really the cause of heavy losses by them later on.

Before leaving Council Grove for Wichita, we made careful inquiry as to the roads, the watering places and thought we would have no trouble in securing water and food, but the trip was so hard and the suffering of the men and horses was so great that I never will forget it. The first day we found the springs and creeks, which we had been told would supply us plenty of water, had dried up and we had great trouble in getting either food or water and but for the fact that we had purchased a lot of hay and put it in the bottom of the wagon for bedding, I don't know what our horses would have done.

We found a place where we could buy water from a well but could get no food for the horses and we stayed there all night. The next day and the following days were worse. The plains were strewn  with the white bones of dead horses and cattle, the sun was hot, and our suffering was great. I really do not see how we stood the trip and several times we were tempted to turn back but Mr. Cooper insisted upon going on. At one place where we were told we would find plenty of water we found a large hole in the bed of a creek that had been dry for weeks. In this hole was some water but the few cattle that were left were standing in it when we drove up and there were dead carcasses of horses and cattle, that had died of hunger and thirst, strewn all over the ground, but it was the only water we could find.

There was plenty of firewood so we built a big fire, carried water out of the hole and boiled it in kettles for ourselves and the horses. There is no use describing the days that followed because every one was about alike. The grain and the grass and the green on the trees had been eaten up by the grasshoppers. The hot winds and weather had dried up the springs and streams and the pioneers had left their homesteads and it is impossible to adequately describe the conditions.

We arrived in Wichita several days later than we had expected and the racing had about ended; it would have been better for us had they been over. Our horses were out of condition and needed days of rest and plenty of care and good feed before they would be ready for racing, but the winning of the race at Council Grove made the owners, who knew but little about the runners, anxious for a race, and on the night we arrived they matched a race between Sleepy Joe and a gray running mare from Missouri called Gray Cow. The race was to come off the next day. When I was told of it I tried to get the owners to let the forfeit go. Joe was in no condition to run, he was leg sore and badly out of condition, but they insisted that Joe could outrun anybody's horse. I saw Mr. Anderson, a livery stable keeper, and the owner of the runner and the stakeholder for the race and told him of the condition of our horses and urged him to talk to the owners, which he did but to no avail. We did prevent them from betting all their money, but they lost what they bet for Joe had no show and was never in the lead from the start to the finish. The loss of the race discouraged the men I was with and their lack of judgement as to the condition of their horses was such that I felt it my duty to give them notice that I would go no further with them.

They started for Texas the next day and I remained in Wichita for the remaining days of the races and secured several good mounts. Before I left I was engaged to ride Little Casino. She was one of the fastest horses in our section of the country but had never been run over six hundred yards. After riding her for a few weeks I told her trainer how we had made Tom a good one-mile horse and Carrie a half mile horse and suggested that we try to make Little Casino run out a full half mile. We began training her with that object in view and as the Kansas people know, she soon became one of the fastest half mile racers.

Racing: Indian Style

We went from Wichita to Topeka by wagon and when we arrived we found that Andrew Wilson, who was known as the Cattle King of Kansas, was preparing to go into the horse business. He had purchased Happy and John Dunning, two trotting horses, and a number of smuggler colts. He already owned Brown Bess. After some days he purchased or arranged to get ahold of Little Casino and I went to work for him.

He had a half mile track on his farm and we began work on his horses to have them ready for the fairs. His cattle were already in good condition. We went to a number of fairs and he took a large number of blue ribbons with his cattle and won a number of races with his horses. While on the farm, he asked me, besides riding the runner, to take the smuggler colt called Witch in hands. She was an outlaw and they said she could kick herself loose from any cart and that she could not be handled. I had a lot of excitement in breaking her. I used ropes and tried the plan of throwing her in the sand and after a few days I had her so she could be harnessed and driven. We could soon ride her and handle her as other horses were handled. She was a good looker but not fast enough for racing.

While working for Wilson, we slept in the barn loft and one night the men discovered that I walked in my sleep. They saw me get up and go down the stairs from the hay mow and enter the stall in which Witch was kept and they watched me rub her and get down in front of her and rub her front legs. They were afraid to wake me for fear the mare would begin kicking. When I left the stall, they woke me up and I could not remember anything I had done.

I quit working for Mr. Wilson in the fall to enter school but soon after starting to school in the late fall of 1874, my grandfather and grandmother Pappan, with a number of other members of the Kaw tribe of Indians, came up to Topeka and while there the men folks induced me to go to their reservation in the Indian Territory with them.

The Government, under an old treaty provision, was issuing rations to members of the tribe. One Saturday I went out on the Little Soldier Creek and caught the little brown mare my mother had left me. She had been running with some semi-wild ponies out northeast of Silver Lake. When my folks were ready to return to the Kaw Reservation in the Indian Territory, I joined them. They had three covered wagons and teams and a number of riding ponies. We expected to reach Wakarusa the first day, but when we reached the six mile creek south of Topeka one of the women was taken sick and that night she gave birth to a baby girl. On account of the condition of the mother and child we were kept in camp on the six mile for several days.

On the day before the party intended to leave for the Territory the men folks had ridden back to Topeka to spend the day, and I had remained in camp with my grandmother, Julie Pappan, a member of the Kaw Tribe by blood. She asked me to come to her wagon and when I arrived she was the only one there. She talked to me a while and asked why I wanted to go to the Indian Territory. When I told her of what the men had said she told me she would like the best in the world to have me at her home but she told me what I might expect on the Indian Reservation and that I would likely become like the most of the men on it; that I would have no schooling, would put in my time riding race horses or ponies, and become a reservation man with no future, and that if I ever expected to make anything of myself I should return to Topeka and start to school again - that as much as she wanted me, because of my dead mother and her love for me, yet for my own good she wanted me to return to Topeka where I could attend the public schools and make somebody of myself.

I took her splendid advice and the next morning as the wagons pulled out for the south, bound for the Indian Territory, I mounted my pony and with my belongings packed in a flour sack, returned to Topeka and to school.

In the winter, I ran short of funds and arranged to work in a livery barn for L. M. Travis for ten dollars per month and board. I was to work nights and mornings and had plenty of time for lessons. I got up at five o'clock every morning with the other stable men; we cleaned out the stable, fed, watered and curried the horses and usually had time to wash up and be ready for an eight o'clock breakfast and to school by nine.

In the spring of 1875, I received a letter from Charles Search of Salina, Kansas asking me my terms for the season to ride two thoroughbreds that had been purchased in Kentucky and were being trained for the summer and fall races in Kansas. I gave them my terms, $50.00 a month and ten percent of the purse winnings of my mounts.

As soon as school was out I went to Salina and there met Charles Search and Colonel Dan Wagstaff and was taken to the stables where

Racing: Indian Style

Tilden, Beecher and Brown Kate were being kept. As I entered the stable door, I heard a noise like that made by a wind sucking horse and looked at the horses to see what was wrong. I discovered that one of the horses, Tilden, was a wind sucker or cribber. I asked what they were doing with a wind sucker and they said they did not know they had one.

After an explanation as to cribbing horses and the effect it had on them, I suggested that we get a strap and I thought we could control the horse. The strap was produced and adjusted.

We did not give the horses a real tryout for several days. One morning bright and early we went to the track for that purpose and after trying Kate and Beecher, I mounted Tilden and gave him a half mile. I had ridden many horses and some of them very fast but when I returned to the stand with Tilden, I told Mr. Search that he was the fastest horse I had ever ridden.

While getting ready for the fair at Salina the chills and fever that had frequently bothered me, as it had others who lived along the rivers and creeks in Kansas in the early days, came on and I was having my regular shake every other day. The fair came on and the day of the big event, the day Tilden was to run his first race, was set and as luck would have it, it was my day for a shake and the owners of the horses were worried because they expected much from Tilden and thought everything depended upon the rider.

There lived in the house nearest the barn an old Irish woman who had a large family of children and took in washing to help support the family. Among others for whom she washed, were the men about our stable. In some way she heard of my having the chills and fever and she told the boss if they would send me over on the last day of my shake before the day of the race, she would cure me.

So, when the day came I went over to her home. She made a cot on the floor, took a lot of blankets, some I think were taken over from the stables, made me put on a night shirt and made me lie down, then she began to prepare the medicine. She rolled a lemon, boiled some coffee, made it good and strong, squeezed the juice of the lemon in a tin cup, then filled it with the hot black coffee, no cream, no sugar, and made me drink it all. It was the bitterest dose I had ever swallowed. Then she covered me with blankets. I perspired a long time. She did not let me up for hours and when I got up I was dry and had no chill and no fever and, for that matter, I have not had a shaking chill since.

When the race came two days later I was in good condition and ready for my mount. Tilden won all the races in which he was entered in the Salina fair. From Salina we went to the various county seat fairs in Kansas, expecting to end the season at Kansas City, Missouri.

My first experience in having two horses from the same stable entered in the same race was at Emporia. In the first half mile race Tilden and Brown Kate were both entered from the Search stable. About noon, I was told that I was to ride Tilden and that I must let Kate win. I told the trainer that I always rode to win and that if I rode Tilden I would win if I could. He said he would see about that.

When the horses were brought out the trainer came to Tilden's head to turn him and handle him. I objected because I had always handled him at the poll myself and did not need any assistance, but I was only a jockey and must submit. I soon discovered the reason for the trainer at my horse's head. I found that his intention was to turn the horse, hold him back and give him a bad start. I protested and told him I could handle the horse. I told it loud enough for the judges to hear. When the word was given, the trainer turned Tilden more than half way around before he let go the bit.

The other horses were off and had nearly reached the first turn before I got Tilden fairly started. I rode for all that was in me, saved every inch and watched every jump. When we entered the back stretch I sent my horse for all he was worth and passed a number of the other horses. As the lead horses struck the lower turn I saw Kate was in the lead, but one of the other horses was making it warm for her and I was gaining on them both. As they entered the home stretch I saw that the other horse was bound to pass Kate, so I threw Tilden far enough toward the middle of the track so as not to bother either of the other horses and urged him to his fastest stride and gained at every jump. As we neared the grand stand, I passed Kate and before reaching the wire I overtook the other horse and won the race by a neck.

The crowd went wild and I was proud of my victory on Tilden and really believe it was the best riding I had ever done. I thought I would be discharged but when we returned to the stable the trainer said nothing and soon the owner, Charles Search (or part owner and manager), came to the stable and instead of dismissing me, he put his hand on my arm and said, "Well, Charley, I have a real race horse and a splendid jockey."

I was pleased in 1920, when at Salina, Kansas to attend a political meeting, to have Reverend Cox tell me that Colonel Dan Wagstaff who was one of the owners of the stable, had told him of the Emporia event, and said he had always been proud of me because I always rode to win.

We took the horses to a number of the fairs, winding up in the state at the State Fair of Topeka. We went from fair to fair overland. We had an experience one day which I think is worth relating. We were on our way to a fair and when we came to the stream we found it was very high. There was no wagon bridge and the water was too deep for us to ford it. I swam with the horses, one by one, over the stream, the last one was Tilden.

I had hardly entered the water when I discovered that Tilden could not or would not swim. I slid off his back, took the bridle reins in my hands and pulled him to the shore which was only a few feet away. There was a railroad bridge near. We went to a farmhouse, got some boards or planks and put them on the ties of the bridge and took Tilden and the wagon across the stream on the railroad bridge.

At Topeka we sold the work horses and wagon, joined with Andrew Wilson, the other owners of horses, and added two trotters and two more runners to our stable. We went from the Topeka fair to fairs in Nebraska.

One day I again found two of the horses in the same race. When I got my saddle ready for Tilden I was advised that I was to ride Kate and the trainer said they wanted her to win. When we lined up for the start I handled Kate and the trainer was at Tilden's head. When we got the word "go" I was off well in front and held the place until we reached the home stretch, then one of the other horses passed me and won by a half-length. Kate was second and Tilden was among the last.

Three days later the same horses were entered in a three-fourths of a mile dash; that day I rode Tilden. I was on the outside, got a good start and led all the way. Tilden had sold in the field in the pools and his owners and backers won a large amount of money. The same day a trotter from our stable, to the surprise of everyone except his owner and backers, won a trotting race and that night Andy Wilson, who owned the trotter and who was backing Tilden for our stable, had every pocket full of mon-

Charles Curtis

ey.

We returned to Topeka from the Nebraska fairs, intending to select a few of our horses to take to Kansas City. When we arrived in Topeka we found that Tilden was sick and the veterinary surgeon said he had lung fever. I was left to look after Tilden and had an agreement that I should spend the nights at the stable with him and could go to school in the day. The horse was sick for several months. When he recovered I took him over to our old barn where we had fine box stalls and a good big yard.

The next year, 1876, we started to the fairs, beginning with the first. When we came to Topeka for the fair in September I entered into an agreement to remain with the stable for another year at $50.00 a month and ten percent of the winnings of my mounts. The fair closed on Saturday. We were to leave for the Kansas City fair on Monday and were to go from there to the Centennial at Philadelphia, then to the Southern Racing Circuit.

On Sunday I went over to visit my grandmother, Permelia Curtis, and told her of my contract. She urged me to give it up and to start to school the next morning. She said if I did not give up riding then I would likely be a rider or a race horse trainer for the remaining years of my life. She said I had saved enough money to pay my school expenses for the next year and that I could make my home with her. She convinced me if I ever intended to get any kind of an education I must give up riding then and start to school at once.

I went back to the grounds that Sunday evening and told Mr. Search, the manager of the stable, of my interview with my Grandmother Curtis. He told me he thought it was the very best advice that I could have and if I wanted to quit the track and go to school that he would release me from my contract and would give me a month's extra pay. After considerable consideration I determined to quit riding and to start to school the next morning. I bade the men and horses goodbye and left the stable that night, went over to my grandmother's home and got ready to enter school. Thus, ending my riding. I had been at it from 1868 and I had been the last two years with Mr. Search and his stable. I had not lost a race with Tilden. I had lost with other horses but always won on the old reliable thoroughbred from Kentucky, Tilden. He was by far the fastest horse I ever rode.

Article No. VI

I quit the track as a rider in September, 1876, but I did not give up horses at that time. My uncle owned a thoroughbred colt called Greely. I began to train him when not in school and soon had him in good condition and running well. I trained him for a year and had him going so fine that he was easily sold.

I started to school on the Monday after being released from my contract with Mr. Search, but in 1877 my money ran low and it looked as though I would be compelled to look for a place but one Saturday while passing the restaurant and bakery of Mr. Weinberger, I noticed some fine apples and oranges in the window. I went in the store, purchased enough applies to fill a small basket, took them home, rubbed them until their skins shone and at train time I went to the Union Pacific Depot and offered my apples for sale to the travelers and they were taken readily and I might say greedily. It was the noon hour and the train stopped for dinner. I was so elated over my success with my first basket of apples that I purchased a barrel that afternoon, had them delivered at the house of my Grandmother Curtis, with whom I was living, and every day at noon I went with apples and oranges to the two trains that stopped for dinner. Once in a while Mr. Weinberger would have oranges which were not going as fast as he liked and he would turn them over to me to sell on shares. I had a good trade and was making money every day, but after about one year the Union Pacific officials, at the request of the hotel management, issued an order against any person peddling or offering fruits, cigars, etc. on the depot platform. I told them if they would let me sell the stock I had on hand I would stop making the trains. This request was granted and my profitable business was at an end.

I had a good time at school but as I had been a race rider and was part Indian I had a good many school boy fights. I soon was in bad with the teachers because of my fighting with the other boys. I tried to lay the blame on the others because they called me the Indian race rider, or the French apple seller but this did not protect me from punishment. The teachers told me I should not notice such things.

The time came when we got a new teacher, T. C. Dick, and while I think he hated to have the boys fighting, yet he seemed to favor me. When I went after the boys for calling me names my punishment was very light and not very often. One day he ended my troubles by a little act which I shall never forget. Just after school took up after the noon hour, he announced that Mr. Curtis would please take charge of the room until he, the teacher, returned. I did as ordered and was in charge the remainder of the day. From that time on I had no trouble. I didn't look for any and the boys seemed to leave me alone. I shall never forget that act of Thomas C. Dick. I really believe it was the best thing that happened to me while attending school.

When my money ran out again I did not know what to do. I wanted to finish school and I must have clothes and books. At last I called upon Mr. Phillips who owned a livery stable. I told him my situation and asked him if he had anything I could do nights and mornings which would enable me to earn enough to keep me in school. He said his business was light; that he already had more men than he needed. He told me he had an old hack, and that a number of his livery teams were idle and if I wanted to try it, he would furnish the hack and team every night and Saturdays and Sundays and I could take it and drive it on shares. He was to keep the hack in repair, furnish the food for the horses and have them hitched and unhitched from the hack whenever I desired. All I had to do was drive when I pleased.

I accepted the offer and that night started out. The hack was old, so old the boys called it Noah's Ark. The trade was light for a few days but we had no street cars, and there was the river to cross to get to the main part of the town, and it seemed a long way between north

Racing: Indian Style

and south Topeka, and when the hotel men and some of the business men found out that I was driving the hack nights to get money to finish school, they became quite liberal and patronized my hack. I soon began to take in from two to six dollars a night and had all the money I needed.

In the summer of 1877 I started to learn the carriage painting trade and entered into a contract with George Wallace, who was one of the best men engaged in that business, but after working at the shop for a month or two, the doctor told me I must give it up because of the effect of the oil, turpentine and other articles used on my health. When I entered the shop, I began in the trade by burning the old paint off buggies, carriages and hacks. After a week or two I was set to work putting on the first coats.

I attended the public schools in Topeka until June, 1879. There were spelling classes, debating societies and other school organizations, all of which I joined and took part in their exercises. In the debating society we settled all the public questions of the day to our own satisfaction, if not to that of the men who were making the laws for the National Government and the various states. At the graduation exercises I was selected to represent one of the classes and I delivered Webster's address on "The Duty of a Chief Magistrate".

It was a great day for us all and when I left the school building that day I really expected to continue until I graduated, but on the way home I was overtaken by Mrs. A. H. Case, the wife of one of the leading lawyers of Kansas. She asked me what I intended to do and I told her I had not made up my mind and she asked me why I did not go to her husband, that she thought he might need a young man in his office.

I talked the matter over with Grandmother Curtis and on the next Monday I called upon Mr. Case. When I called upon him I found that he had been my grandfather's lawyer and he felt quite friendly to the family. He asked what I was doing and I told him that I was driving a hack at night so as to earn enough to pay my expenses and that if I could earn nothing in the office I would keep driving the hack at night until I could earn a living at some other work.

About the end of the conversation, Mr. Case told me that there were too many poor lawyers at the bar. I asked him if there was not room at the top. This seemed to please him and he told me I could come in the next morning. I was to keep the office clean, keep fresh water in the tank and keep the desks, tables, chairs and books dusted and, in the winter, I was to build the fires and I was to be in the office every morning at eight o'clock. I agreed to the terms. I began by reading Blackstone, Kent and other standard law books, and I continued to drive the hack at night and frequently took one of the law books with me which I read while waiting for passengers.

I had not been in the office but a short time when Mr. Case turned some collections over to me; these I was very fortunate in collecting and greatly to my surprise Mr. Case gave me one half of the fees. In a month or two he was sending me to the police courts and a little later he trusted me with cases before Justices of the Peace and he was kind enough and liberal enough to give me part of the fee. In a few months my income was sufficient to justify my giving up hack driving.

I had been in the office but a short time when I learned of the condition of the forty acres of land which my sister, Elizabeth, and I had inherited from our mother. The deed was so poorly drawn that it was doubtful if title passed. A land speculator had secured a quit claim deed and after a number of years in the courts we had been adjudged as having the title, but in 1879 I found that the host of litigation, the survey of the land and the expenses of administration had caused a debt of over $ 5,000.00 to be accumulated. This was secured by mortgage and the taxes for several years back had not been paid.

In 1879, I had the right of majority conferred and took charge of the property for my sister and myself. I tried but was unable to make a new loan so I arranged to sell lots and pay a certain amount of the purchase money to the holder of the mortgage. I sold one-quarter of a block of land to a distillery and gave them one-quarter of a block. I did the same with a brewery and had a distillery and a brewery located in the southwest corner of the land. After this was done, it was easy to sell lots on monthly payments and I turned the payments over to the bankers and soon had the mortgage and back taxes paid and after this was done I began to build small houses on the lots.

Every lot was properly surveyed and staked, but when I had sold the lots in one block running to the river I found that the purchasers had fenced over their lines to the extent that when the river was reached there was one lot short. As luck would have it, some of the purchasers had bought two or three lots so all that was needed was to move a few fences.

In 1879 when the colored refugees were brought to Kansas from the South, a large number of them were landed in Topeka. They came without money, had no property, there was no place for them to stay and there was but little if any work for them. They were in such condition that a Freedmans Relief Association was organized to take care of them and I gave permission for them to use timber and build dugouts on a part of the forty acres of land owned by my sister, Elizabeth, and me. This act of kindness was never forgotten by the colored people and their descendants and they have been my friends and supporters ever since.

We organized a home talent theatrical company and put on plays for the benefit of churches and other organizations on the north side. The plays were well patronized at home. The temperance question was up in the state as Governor St. John had recommended a Constitutional amendment on the subject and one of our leading plays was "Ten Nights in a Barroom". We put on "The Hidden Hand" and many other leading plays of the day.

The truth is we thought we had a great company and after putting on a few plays we were ready to tackle most anything. After a few weeks we arranged to go to some of the small towns and were quite successful for a time, but like all companies, we wanted to take in the larger cities in our state and we had poor days and nights, but the worst was at Lawrence, Kansas. We were billed for a night show there and the prospects for a big house were fine: we went down on the morning train and found that up to noon about $60.00 worth of the tickets had been sold and all predicted that the Opera House would be crowded, but about three o'clock it began to snow and it fell thick and fast. By opening time, a regular blizzard was on. We were stopping at the Planters Hotel which was just across the street from the Opera House, and at the proper time, we went on but there were only about twenty-five people in the audience. We considered for some time as to what we better do. We had but little money and needed the box receipts so we concluded to go on with the play and did. The small crowd seemed to enjoy it but most of us behind the footlights were worried. When the show was over we found we had enough money to pay the rent for the House but not enough to pay our hotel bill and railroad tickets home. So, we went to the proprietor of the hotel and borrowed enough money from him to get our troupe home. Most of us went up on the caboose of a freight and got home for breakfast a tired, disgusted and disappointed crowd.

My first tailored suit was an interesting experience. After I entered the law office of Mr. Case and was taking in enough money to afford a tailor-made suit I ordered one from a man on the north side who had boarded at my grandmother's and whom I knew quite well. A few days before the suit was to be ready I received a telegram calling me to Iowa because of the serious illness of my sister, Elizabeth. I called on the tailor and told him I must have the suit in time to leave on the afternoon train and he promised to have it ready. The suit was delivered at the house and just before train time I put it on. The coat and vest were all right but the trouser legs were so short that I had to stuff them in my boot tops.

Racing: Indian Style

I hadn't time to get a pair of trousers at the store and so started on the trip. The trouser legs were so short that I could not put one knee over the other without the trouser legs coming out over the boot top, and so I had a time of it until I arrived in the Iowa town.

I arrived there late and all the stores were closed. There were a number of daughters at the home of my brother-in-law, and they had young lady and gentlemen callers the night I arrived and I had a bad few hours. When I explained my troubles in the morning and asked to be directed to a good store where I could buy me a pair of trousers, the family had a good laugh at my expense.

In 1880 my sister Elizabeth and her husband concluded they wanted to move to Las Vegas, New Mexico and I sold a number of small houses and lots to raise the money they needed.

I continued to try cases in the Justice and Police courts while I was studying law. The work in the Police Courts was of little value but I found my experience before Justices of the Peace of great assistance. Many questions of law were raised, argued and passed upon and the presentation of the question raised was as full and elaborate, if not as able, as it would have been in the higher courts.

I remember being employed to try a case before a Justice of the Peace at Muscotah, Kansas; that was just before I was admitted to practice in the District Courts. I raised a constitutional question and the Justice sustained my point. The old lawyers poked a lot of fun at the Justice and me but upon appeal the same point was made and the Justice was sustained in the higher courts.

I was admitted to the bar in June, 1881. The day I took the examination before W. P. Douthitt, M. T. Campbell and H. C. Safford, the committee appointed by the court to examine me, I left Topeka for a month's vacation in New Mexico.

Just before leaving Mr. Case called me into his room and after talking with me a few minutes and asking me about my intended trip, he told me not to get stuck on any of the towns I visited because he wanted me to return as soon as I could and that I might know what I had in front of me. He said he would give me a one-third interest; that is, the firm would be Case and Curtis, he to have two-thirds of all the fees collected and I was to have one-third. I gladly accepted at once and upon my return found the new sign, Case and Curtis, Attorneys at Law, hanging beside his old sign of A.H. Case, Attorney at Law. The new letterheads were printed and we were all ready for business.

Soon after I entered the law office of Mr. Case he gave me advice which I never forgot. There was a small case assigned to me to look after and I asked Mr. Case about the law. He told me it would be best for me to look it up for myself. He said, "Go to the Revised Statutes and if you don't find all you want there, look it up in the standard works on the subject." He said it was always better for one to look up the questions than to depend upon the judgement or advice of others. I never forgot the splendid advice and ever since that day it has been a rule of mine to study questions for myself and not depend upon others for information.

My experience in the Justice Courts had been so great that I had but little trouble handling cases in the District Courts. Mr. Case had a large practice and many of his cases were outside of our home county. My first case was in the District Court at Abilene. Here I had my first experience with unethical lawyers. I had filed a motion in the case but did not know that the Judge took up motions on certain days. A few days before the opening of the court our firm received a card from the attorneys on the other side that the case would not be reached before Wednesday of the following week and so I arranged to go up at that time, but when I arrived, I found that Tuesday was motion day and that the attorneys on the other side had insisted that the motion be argued.

A young lawyer, Mr. Close, a friend, happened to be in the courtroom and when he saw what was going on, explained to the court that I was absent and asked that the motion go over until he could communicate with me, but the other side objected and the court took up the motion. My friend, after going over the papers, told the court that he would represent me and he argued my motion and the court sustained it.

When I arrived the next morning (Wednesday), I was advised as to what had happened. I had all office papers with me and I showed the card to Mr. Close and the Court. There was some talk of disbarment proceedings against the lawyers on the other side but because of the age of one of the members of the firm the matter was not pushed.

Article No. VII

When I began the study of law I had no intention of ever taking a hand in the political game. I remembered that while my Grandfather Curtis was an ardent and active Republican, he had no desire to hold office and was never a candidate, although he was often urged to make the race for the State Legislature or other local offices. Many may think it was very strange that he had no political ambitions when they learn that he was a citizen of Indiana for many years.

I had been in the law office of Mr. Case, who had been a follower of Jim Lane, but a short time before he told me of his experience in politics and he advised me to keep out, at least so far as being a candidate and I concluded the best thing for a young lawyer to do was to keep out.

But when asked to join the Republican Flambeau Club in 1880 I could not resist. This club had more than a state-wide reputation and had won the applause of the people in many sections of the state. All knew that if the Topeka Flambeau Club was to be on hand there would be a grand torch light procession and plenty of fireworks. I joined and with the other young Republicans put on an oil cloth cap, carried a torch and helped shoot off the fire works. We had lots of fun and "the bee" for office did not sting me and in fact I heard none of its "buzzings." I was content to march in the mud, holler myself hoarse, burn my hands and neck and scorch my hair with the torch or the accidental discharge of some of the pieces of fire works, and I perspired as only one can who carries a torch and marches miles in a political campaign. When the Topeka Flambeau Club was to furnish the red fire and the Modocs of Topeka were to sing, a

Charles Curtis

wonderful time was always assured.

One afternoon in April, 1884, a boy came running into our law office and told me I was wanted immediately at the voting place in the First Ward. I asked him what was up and he told me they were voting for delegates, that I was on the ticket and there was a hard fight going on. I went over at once and found a real live contest was on. The active Republicans were at the polls and they were divided up in little groups, many were talking loudly but no man who came up to vote escaped. He was buttonholed at once by the contending forces and was vigorously urged to vote one ticket and then the other. It usually ended in the voter taking all the tickets offered and his voting the one he pleased when he came to cast his ballot.

We had no Australian ballot law then and each set of candidates got up their own tickets and they and their friends saw that they were printed and supplied in sufficient numbers for all the voters.

I did not know at first what it was all about, but as my name was on one of the tickets, I at once got busy urging my neighbor to vote "our ticket." When the votes were counted it was found that our ticket had been successful and a delegation had been selected from the First Ward and I had received some three hundred sixty more votes than had been cast for James A. Troutman, a leader of the prohibition element. I was informed that the delegates selected were to attend a county convention to elect delegates to a state convention which was to select delegates to the Republican National Convention.

Our delegation met to organize and Honorable W. S. Stambaugh was made chairman and Honorable L. F. Eggers was selected as his assistant. These two men were old and experienced in the political game, had been active in the celebrated Ingalls investigation of a few years before and had moved to Topeka after the investigation because they thought the Capitol City offered them a better political future than the small communities in which they lived before the Ingalls Investigation. It was stated that Mr. Stambaugh was anxious to become Probate Judge and that Mr. Eggers had his eye on the office of Prosecuting Attorney (County Attorney) for Shawnee County.

But there was one D. C. Metsker who had made and unmade county offices and dictated delegates to conventions for years. It was claimed that one could get but little recognition in a political way in the city or county unless he had the backing of Mr. Metsker.

The convention met on a Saturday morning, April 21 or 22, 1884. Mr. Metsker and his followers won out for the temporary organization and the convention adjourned until 2 p.m. While we were all agreed that we would send a delegation to the State Convention favorable to Colonel George R. Peck of Topeka as one of the delegates to the Republican National Convention, yet we were not agreed as to whom should be delegates to the State Convention.

The prohibition sentiment was strong in the state. The Constitutional amendment had been adopted in 1880 and Colonel Peck desired to select his own delegates and because of the prominence of the Temperance question, he was anxious to have James A. Troutman named as one of the delegates, for Mr. Troutman was one of the leaders in the prohibition movement; was a strong man and had a large following in various sections of the state.

It was known that when the time came to select the delegates there would be a battle royal and the Court House was filled with a crowd about evenly divided, and all anxious for the contest to begin. When our delegation gathered at two, neither Stambaugh nor Eggers were on hand. Their alternates were in the Courtroom and took their places and as I was the only lawyer remaining on the delegation from the First Ward, I was selected to act as the Chairman until Stambaugh or Eggers returned, but for some reason they did not come back.

It was my first convention and I did not know what to do nor how or when to do it. The reports of the Committees were called, for the temporary organization was made permanent. At last the report of the committee on delegates was presented and then the fun began. They had suggested the name of Mr. Troutman for the First Ward and my delegation told me to fight, and so I moved to strike his name from the list and to substitute another for it. My contention was that at the election in the First Ward his name was on the ticket and had been defeated and that we who had won the contest had a right to one of our choices on the delegation. The convention sustained my contention, then someone from the Fourth Ward withdrew in his favor and I succeeded in defeating that motion and then they tried to put him on from one of the precincts outside the city; this I opposed and was successful. The fight lasted all afternoon and when the convention finally adjourned, those who had helped in the fight were wild with joy. I remember that they hardly let my feet touch a step of the stairs upon leaving the Courthouse, they virtually carried me down the stairs and nearly everyone on our side was saying that I must be a candidate for County Attorney.

The following is taken from the local press which devoted a lot of space to the report of the county convention and in commenting on the failure of the older men to control it, one of them said: "When it comes to running a convention, however, they must admit that 'Charles Curtis is a devilish smart boy.' Another said, "If they let Charlie Curtis fudge, however, with the reckless audacity he displayed in the convention, they will view the interesting campaign from the gallery while the parquet seats are checked off to Quinton, Ensminger and others." Another said, "Attorney Vance was in the late convention, Mayor Miller was in the late convention, and so was Joab Mulvane and others, and they did what they could to protect the cause and help out Mr. Troutman. They looked vacantly one at the other, gazing silently into the deep recesses of their hats and thought of the adage, "God helps those that help themselves. In the meantime, Charley Curtis was helping himself".

I rejected to oppose Mr. Troutman, he and I were friends and had been for several years, we had attended the same school but I was young and thought I had to carry out the wishes of the delegates from our ward. The County Attorney was to be elected in November and the county convention would not be held for several months. I told all I had no desire to be elected County Attorney; our firm had all the law business it could look after and that my income was more than the fees and the salary of the office would amount to. The County Attorney was paid a salary of two thousand per year and was allowed certain fees in case of conviction where the costs were paid by the defendant, and he was also allowed a per cent on all money recovered for the county.

There was not a day passed that did not find from five to ten voters of the county calling at our office to urge me to become a candidate. They contended I was the only man in the county who could break the Metsker slate and the only man in the party who could be elected. I told them I was ready to help organize so that no one man could dictate the nominees for the various county offices and I did help make an organization of fifty-nine young men taken from different wards in the city and

Racing: Indian Style

townships in the county who agreed to fight to win the county from the man or men who then controlled the conventions. We agreed that when any member of our organization became a candidate that he should withdraw from the organization, but that he might name the Republican voter to take his place. We met once a week and oftener on call.

At every meeting of the organization there was full attendance and at every meeting it was insisted by many of the members that I must become a candidate for County Attorney. The pressure became so great that I took the matter up with my partner; at first he advised me to keep out but one day after a member had called he said it would be a great experience for me; that I would be engaged in trial of cases nearly all the time and that while the fees and salary would not amount to as much as I was getting as my share of the income of the firm, that the experience would be more than enough to compensate me for the loss and he advised me to go in, stating that if elected I could fill out my term and then go back to the general practice. When the next delegation called I told them I would give them an answer within a week.

The truth was I had no desire to become a candidate. I talked with my folks at home. My grandmother who had helped me so much, thought it would be a good thing for me to do, and by the end of the week my friends had induced me to enter the race. I told the committee when they called that I had made up my mind to enter the contest, if they would agree to help me organize the county, and on June 25, 1884, I announced my candidacy.

At the next meeting of our little organization I announced that I had consented to make the race for County Attorney and withdrew from the organization. The members all wished me well and the contest was on. Mr. Crumrine, who had been a partner of the County Attorney, announced and was at once recognized as the candidate of the Metsker organization and of the dry forces.

I showed considerable strength, within a week or two, in the north part of the county where I had been born and raised. The Metsker people thought it would be a good plan to bring out a candidate against me from the north side and so they induced M. T. Campbell to announce. He had lived in North Topeka for a number of years, enjoyed a good practice, and was a lawyer of high standing. His announcement made some trouble for me, as it caused Mr. J. S. Ensminger, who was recognized as a resubmissionist and was a young lawyer of ability and several years' experience, to announce his candidacy. This divided our forces while their people were working together. I knew that their delegate would support either Mr. Crumrine or Mr. Campbell, whomever they thought the stronger, and I was convinced that Mr. Ensminger was in to stay, for it had been his desire to be a candidate from the first.

I had a team of small black ponies, they were fine drivers, used to the road, and I kept them on the go until election day. I knew my friends would look after the wards in Topeka and it was my desire to secure as many delegates as possible from outside the city, so I visited every neighborhood.

When the delegates were elected it was found that no one of us had enough delegates to be nominated on the first ballot, but Mr. Ensminger and I had more than enough to nominate one of us if we could combine and I had a few more delegates than he. The County Convention met August 16, 1884. Mr. Campbell withdrew and his delegates announced for Mr. Crumrine. While one half of the County Officers were to be nominated at the convention and delegates were to be selected for the Republican State Convention, yet all the fight was centered in the office of County Attorney. It was perfectly apparent that there would be a deadlock unless Mr. Ensminger and I reached some kind of agreement, and if we both remained before the convention too long the delegates might get tired and nominate Mr. Crumrine. He had the Metsker organization and all the dry forces back of him and his delegates were mostly old men in the game, while many of our delegates were just beginners. At last and just a few minutes before the convention, Mr. Ensminger and I had a meeting with a few of our friends to see if we could not reach some kind of agreement that would enable our delegates to vote for one of us on the first ballot. I insisted that as I had more delegates than he that is was his duty to withdraw.

He admitted that I would have more votes than he on the first ballot but he was an older man and had been at the bar longer than I had and that he would gain strength on every ballot after the first and he was quite sure that I would lose votes after the first ballot. I asked him upon what ballot he thought he would take the lead and he said the second, and not later than the third. I told him if he had that much confidence I would agree that the one of us having the fewest votes at the end of the

Racing: Indian Style

third ballot should withdraw. This he agreed to. This information was given to our delegates.

When the roll was closed on the first ballot Mr. Crumrine lead with forty-two votes, I was second with twenty-five votes and Ensminger was third with twenty-four votes. On the second ballot the vote stood Crumrine forty-one votes, Curtis twenty-five votes and Ensminger twenty-five votes with no choice. The third ballot was Crumrine thirty-nine votes, Curtis thirty-one votes and Ensminger twenty-two votes. I not only lead Mr. Ensminger on the third ballot but had gained votes, but he refused to withdraw.

His delegates who knew of the arrangement insisted that he keep the agreement. This he refused to do and the fourth vote of the convention was soon on and soon over. The vote stood Curtis forty-eight votes, Crumrine forty-four votes. I had secured the nomination. The convention went wild for a few minutes.

I thought and so did my friends that when the nomination was secured that the fight was really over because Shawnee County was strongly Republican and a nomination on the Republican ticket was equivalent to an election, but we were soon aware that the fight had just begun. The Prohibition Republicans were displeased with the nomination of Dr. S. E. Sheldon for State Senator and with my nomination as County Attorney. And they brought out, as independent candidates, Honorable A. L. Williams, one of the leading lawyers and ablest men in the State for State Senator, and Judge William P. Douthit as an independent candidate for County Attorney.

Mr. Williams was a Kansas pioneer and general attorney for the Union Pacific Railway Company and strong and knew nearly every man in the county: in fact, he was one of the best-known men in the state. Judge Douthit was one of the oldest and one of the leading members of the bar. These two men had plenty of means of their own and the temperance people opened headquarters for them and began an active and thorough campaign.

They also began a fight on Dr. Sheldon and me before the Republican County Central Committee. They charged us with most everything and had us called before the County Central Committee to show cause why our names should not be taken from the Republican County ticket. The contest became hot and exciting, our opponents had a majority on the county ticket but as we had both been fairly nominated, the County Committee, after several meetings, determined to leave our names on the ticket.

We opened headquarters and started a regular school house campaign. It was interesting from the start to the finish, and so close to make it very exciting. I shall never forget the first meeting. It was at Wakarusa, a strong temperance neighborhood, but among the older men there were a large number of Union soldiers, almost all of whom were radical Republicans. At this meeting I paid my respects to some of those who were opposing Dr. Sheldon and me.

Some who had been for us in the primaries were opposing us. I questioned their motives. I insisted that the prohibitory law had not been enforced and I promised if elected that my best efforts would be put forth in its enforcement; that it was the law and should be obeyed and enforced as other laws. On the way home, the other candidates jumped all over me for naming those Republicans who were fighting us. They told me that "molasses would catch more flies than vinegar," etc., etc. But I kept up my fight. My object was to get the Republicans who were opposing Dr. Sheldon and me out into the open and this I succeeded in doing before the campaign was over.

In some neighborhoods I had some interesting experiences. There was one meeting which I shall never forget. It was at Lux Schoolhouse. We were to take supper with Phillip Lux; when we arrived at his house he was very cordial to the two speakers (they were old campaigners) who were with me, but he turned me over to the young folks. I thought at first it was because of my age (I was only 24), but when the meeting opened I soon discovered that he was strongly opposed to my candidacy. He introduced the other speakers in glowing terms; told his neighbors he was proud to introduce such strong temperance men, etc. He held me off until the last and when he presented me to the audience, he had something to say because I was not a prohibitionist and he called upon me to explain my position.

He was really so rough that he drove the crowd to me. I told the audience that thousands of dollars had been expended; that spotters had been employed and used and yet the law had not been enforced; that there were then (in 1884) nearly one hundred open saloons in Topeka and that it looked as if the prohibitionists could not enforce it and that while I did not believe in the law, if elected I would put forth every effort to enforce it and that I would at least do as well as those in office had done, and that I believed the law should be enforced, that the only way to tell whether the law was good or bad was to enforce it and then the people would know whether they wanted it or not.

We had hardly driven out of the gate until one of the two speakers said to the other one, "Well, Judge, would you like a drink?" He said he had brought a bottle along thinking it might be a little chilly going home. They soon emptied the bottle and then the Judge informed the Colonel that he had a bottle and before we arrived home they had used up their two bottles. I did not drink and because of my treatment by Mr. Lux, the joke seemed to be on me; at least, my two spellbinder friends thought it was. It was so good that they told it to the boys around the Courthouse and it soon got back to Mr. Lux, and after I was elected and had succeeded in closing the saloons he came into my office to tell me how sorry he was for his conduct at the meeting and from then on he was one of my warmest friends and strongest supporters.

The nearer we got to election day the hotter the campaign grew and one day the report came that the Prohibition Campaigners were taking up collections at their meetings: this was just what I wanted them to do because both Douthit and Williams were rich men and when I secured the positive proof, I made that one of my issues and as the people of the county knew both men to be rich the new turn was of great help to Dr. Sheldon and me. On election night the returns were announced between sets from the stage of the Grand Opera House. Dr. Sheldon and I were both elected.

Article No. VIII

Annie E. Baird, daughter of John and Jane Baird of North Topeka, and I had gone to the same public school, we had attended the same church and Sunday School for years and we had agreed to be married on Thanksgiving Day, 1884.

We went to a show in the Grand Opera House on the night of the election. It had been given out that the election returns would be announced from the stage. When the votes from some of the precincts were announced I was sorry that I had taken Miss Baird with me, but when the final announcement was made showing the election of the entire ticket, I was pleased that she had gone with me.

We were married November 27, 1884, and lived happily together until her passing, June 20, 1924. There came to add to our joy and happiness three children, Permelia, Harry and Leona. Mrs. Curtis lived to see them married and in their homes.

I took charge of the office of County Attorney on the 12th of January, 1885. When I took over the office I found how much systematic work in an office helped. Under arrangement with the outgoing County Attorney, all cases in which I was **(not)** interested were to be disposed of in December. As soon as these cases were out of the way I began to study the cases which would come up in January (1885) term.

I was surprised when the County Attorney advised me he kept no office docket and had no memoranda of pending cases. I called upon my Clerk of the District Court and we went over the docket and very much to my surprise I found 108 criminal cases on the docket for the January term. I briefed each case both as to the law and facts and noted the names of witnesses. Before the Court opened every case on the criminal docket was ready for trial so far as the state was concerned.

The term of my predecessor ran over by one week into the new term of the court and the then presiding judge held over one week. At the request of the County Attorney I took charge of all the criminal cases at the opening of the court. A number of criminal cases were tried the first week but nothing of great interest occurred. The old judge (Judge John Martin) was to retire at the end of the week, and as the Grand Jury had been drawn upon his orders, the lawyers were delaying their motions for the new Judge.

When court opened for the second week with a new Judge (John Guthrie), the lawyer for the defendants filed their various motions to quash and pleas in abatement. The main fight was upon the legality of the drawing of the grand jury who had returned the indictments. The ablest lawyers at the Topeka Bar; A. H. Case, Judge W. C. Webb, A. L. Williams, Dave Overmyer, Capt. J. G. Waters, William P. Douthit and others represented the various defendants, but Case and Webb were selected to lead the fight for the defendants and I alone represented the state. These men were the leaders of the bar, old and tried lawyers, but I had been in cases where the same questions had been raised and I was confident my position would be sustained, but to make sure that I would overlook nothing, a few weeks before court opened I went to the State Library and read every decision I could find on the questions which would be raised by the various motions. I put in all the time I could spare for three weeks at this work. When the motions came up for argument I was fully prepared; the questions were argued for about a week, at the end of which the Court decided in my favor.

Judge Webb paid me quite a compliment after the court handed down its opinion. He said that he had been practicing law for many years and had raised and argued many questions, but he never before had met a lawyer on the other side who had anticipated every question he raised and point he intended to make.

The following are a few of the newspaper comments on the hearing of the motion.

Racing: Indian Style

THE NEW COUNTY ATTORNEY

1-15-1885

Mr. Chas. Curtis, the new County Attorney, made an argument yesterday morning in the District Court in reply to the argument made by the counsel for defendants in the whiskey cases, on their plea in abatement against the indictments found by the grand jury. It was Mr. Curtis' first important speech since becoming County Attorney and he agreeably surprised his friends by the force and strength of his address and his fearless condemnation of lawlessness. Mr. Curtis will have the support and encouragement of all law abiding citizens in the straightforward and manly course he has marked out in his first official utterances.

1-31-1885

There were some wonderful arguments made by the attorneys for the liquor men yesterday. County Attorney Curtis covered every point and made it exceedingly warm for the violators, and required only three-fourths of an hour in which to do it.

Topeka Mail and Breeze

February 20, 1885

A good many straight prohibitionists in Shawnee County announce themselves agreeably disappointed in the notions of County Attorney Curtis. The rapid manner in which Charley has put the forces of the saloonists to flight must be surprising to a good many people who anticipated something else.

After the question as the legality of the Grand Jury had been settled, I had to determine in what order I would try the cases. My predecessor had always prosecuted the small violators first, men without money, the class who were unable to employ the best lawyers and I knew this course caused much criticism. I concluded the better plan would be to pick out the richest and most prominent violators of the law to try first. I selected the case against Frank Durein as the first to be tried.

I shall never forget that trial. I had mapped out my course and intended to follow it. A. H. Case, W. C. Webb, and others were defending. We put in most of the first day selecting a jury. A committee of fifteen who favored the enforcement of the prohibitory liquor law had been selected to visit the Courthouse and watch the proceedings. When the jury was finally accepted by both sides, it was composed of seven resubmissionists and five prohibitionists. I had not exercised a single peremptory challenge of a Juror.

When the makeup of the jury was known, the committee of fifteen filed out of the courtroom and spread the news. They said it was evident that the new County Attorney, Charlie Curtis, did not intend to enforce the law, because he had neglected to use any of his peremptory challenges, and that the jury was made up of seven against five for the law.

The morning after the jury was drawn a member of the Board of County Commissioners called upon me and told me of the reports and said the Board would be glad to employ Judge John Martin to assist me. I thanked him but told him I did not need assistance in the trial of the cases and that the Board need not employ Judge Martin or any other lawyer to assist me and that if I could not handle the cases properly and fully protect the interest of the state that I would resign.

We were two days trying the first case and as soon as the jury went out I had the next case called, which was against Mr. Kreipe. The jury reported in about fifteen minutes that they had reached an agreement. They were brought into the courtroom and the verdict was read, and it disclosed that the defendant had been found guilty on seven counts, all that were in the indictment. This being the first conviction which had been had for some time the news spread fast and the verdict was the talk of the town.

I asked one of the jurors, a resubmissionist, who was a warm friend of mine, what had kept the Jury out so long and he said they were looking for more counts upon which to find the defendant guilty. The lawyer for Mr. Kreipe asked that we delay completing the jury in his case until morning, stating that they thought we could save time. To this I agreed, having a good idea of what would happen in the morning, and it did happen. They offered to plead guilty to one count if the court would assess a fine only. This I refused to accept but did accept the plea of guilty on all the counts.

The conviction of Durein and the plea of guilty of Kreipe was the beginning of the end. But I kept up my plan and called the cases just as fast as I could, always taking the wealthiest and most prominent violators first. I sent a notice to everyone, charged or suspected, that the prosecutions would continue as long as the saloons were running. In a couple of weeks there were eighteen men in the county jail and that many more waiting sentence. The jail would not hold any more.

The Topeka Daily Capitol of February 4, 1885, had the following to say about the prohibition law in Topeka.

> "There are eighteen saloon keepers in jail, retained there because they refuse to pay their fines. They have been very hilarious, singing songs, telling stories and ordering good meals which, under the rules of the jail, all prisoners are permitted to do. Our gin-singing friends have taken their captivity as a joke and have had a merry time of it. The stories will soon all be told, the jokes exhausted, and those lawbreakers will realize that there is a serious side to their present situation. It will dawn on them gradually that being in jail as lawbreakers is not all funny, that very few people in the community are helping them laugh, and that down in the hearts of even the people who drank over their counters there is little sympathy. The sober thought that will come to these saloon keepers is that the law backed by the power of the state beats the transgressor, that sooner or later it comes to crush the individual who believed himself safe amidst the technicalities, evasions and appeals of his legal counsellors. The saloon keepers have had their laugh and maudlin joke over the law that cannot be enforced, and yet eighteen of those men look out through the iron bars of the county jail, they know better than anybody in Topeka, that the law is enforced.
> Judge Guthrie has stood squarely for the enforcement of the law and without fear of favor has simply done his duty as a "just judge."
> Of the new county attorney, Mr. Charles Curtis, from whom the saloon keepers have expected favors because he is not a prohibitionist, it is just to say he has done his official duty as any honest officer ought to do."

On the night of February 15, 1885, just a month and three days after I took my oath of office, the last saloon closed its doors and there were no more open saloons in Topeka during the four years I was County Attorney, except a place was opened one morning during the big State Fair but I had it closed within a few hours and the Sheriff had possession of all their whiskey and beer.

Before I took hold of the office of Prosecuting Attorney there had been a committee of temperance men who had collected a fund with which to gather information against the violators of the Prohibitory Liquor laws. They had employed detectives or spotters. I, as County Attorney, advised the committee that I would not use their spotters as witnesses and that so far as my office was concerned, that they might as well dismiss the men they had employed and during my four years in office I did not place a spotter on the stand and the committee was not called upon to assist in any way.

In the first year I did not lose a single liquor case. There was $5,000 collected in funds which were turned into the school fund, and the county of Shawnee was not called upon to pay cost in such cases to exceed one hundred dollars. After I closed the saloons I began prosecutions against the joints which opened up in various parts of the city, then the drug stores and last the clubs, but after the saloons were closed we were after the bootleggers all the time.

When I took the office, I found every Justice Court was busy almost every day trying disturbances of the peace cases. I issued an order that no petty cases of that kind should be brought without the complaint being filed by the County Attorney. When people called to complain in such cases they were told that if their cases failed they would be held for cost. It was not long before the courts were free of disturbance of the peace cases, and the cost of criminal prosecution was very materially reduced. I remember the county auditor (J. G. Wood) asked me how much would be needed to pay cost in criminal cases for the year. I asked him what they had expended the year before and he said over three thousand dollars. I told him to put down fifteen hundred dollars for the next year. There was less than one thousand expended.

During the time I was Prosecuting Attorney I lost four criminal cases the first year, one the second year and none the last two years and I did not lose a single case during the prohibitory liquor law in the four years. One thing which spoke well for prohibition is the fact that while for years the court docket at every term of court had been crowded with all kinds of criminal cases for trial, there was one term of court, after the law had been enforced for two or three years and the saloons and joints had been closed, that there was not a single criminal case on the docket for trial; that was the September term, 1887. There were some criminal cases on the docket but they were cases of suspended sentences or matters of that kind. Between the time I was admitted to the bar in 1881 and my election to Congress in 1892, eleven years, I was employed for the defense or the prosecution in twenty-eight murder cases.

One day I was sitting at my desk when a gentleman entered the office. He said he was looking for a lawyer by the name of Charles Curtis. I told him that was my name and he said, "You are too young, you cannot be the man I am looking for." I told him that I was the only Charles Curtis at the Topeka Bar. He shook his head and said, "You are too young. You are nothing but a boy." He further stated that he was from Ohio and that he was interested in an important law suit and he had been advised to employ Charles Curtis or Captain J. B. Johnson. I told him Captain Johnson was one of the oldest and best lawyers in Topeka and that his office was just a block up the street and I would send the janitor to direct him to the Captain's office.

The next morning my friend returned, he told me he had employed Captain Johnson, but that after he had made the arrangement, the Captain told him he had better employ me to assist him in the preparation and trial of the case and he was there to retain me, if I cared to help in the case. I told him it would be a pleasure to be in the case with Captain Johnson, but when I told him what my fee would be, he said that was more than he was paying the man he wanted me to help. I told him that would be my fee. He paid me a retainer and I tried the case.

This incident is related because it was what caused me to let a mustache grow. I was then considered tall and slim and weighed about 125 pounds. I started a mustache the next day and it has been growing ever since.

Article No. IX

There was one occurrence in the trial of a liquor case before a Justice of the Peace which I feel like telling about. Under the laws of Kansas anyone could file a complaint before a Justice of the Peace in a misdemeanor case. One day I had a hurry call to go before a justice to try a liquor case. I went to the Courtroom and found a large crowd and they seemed to be having a good time. Witnesses were swearing that they had called for and obtained "shagerach" and they did not know what it was or that they had asked for and received cold tea and they did not know what it was and the assistant in the court who was trying the case was unable to get anything definite from the witnesses.

As soon as I entered the room there was a lull in the proceedings until I took charge of the case. I looked over the list of witnesses and found on it the name of an old colored man whom I had known for years and I was satisfied that he would tell the truth and I called him to the stand.

I asked the usual preliminary questions and then asked the witness if he had purchased anything to drink from the defendant. He said he had purchased what they called "cold tea." I asked him what it was and he said, "It was the hottest whiskey I ever swallowed." I asked him if he had purchased any other liquor and he said he had bought something they called "de shagerach." I asked him what it was and he said it was the best lager beer he had ever swallowed. I asked him to tell the court and jury who was in the room at the time. He named a few men and stopped, I asked him to go on and name the others.

Racing: Indian Style

He turned to the Justice and asked if he must tell, the Justice told him it was a proper question and he should answer. He turned his back to the Justice, pointed his thumb over his shoulder and said, "He was dah, he was dah." The crowd had a good laugh at the expense of the Justice and after examining a few more witnesses the case went to the jury and a verdict of guilty was returned.

There are so many things that happen in one's life that help or hurt and many times they come in very unexpected ways. I feel justified in relating one case which I think caused me to be employed in so many murder cases.

Soon after I was admitted to the bar and taken into the firm we were employed to defend a man charged with murder. There was nothing strange in that because A. H. Case was one of the greatest criminal lawyers this country has ever produced and I think in his day he was the greatest trial lawyer in the west - surely he was the leading trial lawyer in Kansas. He asked me to go up to the preliminary hearing, take full notes of the testimony (we had no court reporters in the western courts then), ask any questions I thought best but not put the defendant on the stand. We knew our client would be bound over.

I attended the hearing and the defendant was bound over to the District Court. When I reported the preliminary hearing to Mr. Case I told him that if one of the witnesses gave the same evidence at the trial in the District Court that he gave at the preliminary hearing, that our client would likely be convicted of manslaughter in the fourth degree; that the witness was one of the defendant's best friends and he had volunteered the statement; that it had not been drawn from him by questions and was not made in answer to a direct question; that the statement being so made I thought it best not to emphasize it and so had not cross-examined the witness. Mr. Case asked me to go to the jail with him to review the case with the defendant and that he wanted me to tell the defendant of the damaging nature of the evidence of his friend and repeat to our client what my notes showed.

We went over to see the defendant a few days later and when, in the review of the evidence we reached the witness, I told him of the statement that had been volunteered and how dangerous it was to him. He said the witness was mistaken and that as he was one of his best friends he knew he would not repeat the statement at the trial, unless it was brought out by a direct question and he felt sure he could convince him he was mistaken and hoped he would be able to get him to correct the statement, if asked about it.

A few days later the defendant secured a bond and was released from jail. Soon after, he told us that he had talked with his friend and that while his friend insisted that the matter mentioned by him had happened, but he would not repeat it at the trial unless asked a direct question on the subject.

The trial came on. We were getting on nicely until the witness, whose statement we feared, was put on the stand. He was asked a question or two by the County Attorney and then he was asked to state what happened. He related a story substantially as he had at the preliminary hearing, repeating the dangerous part, and we knew it was bad for our client, if taken advantage of by the Prosecuting Attorney. This happened about noon and Mr. Case asked for a recess until two o'clock and that the cross-examination be proceeded with at that time.

The court met at two o'clock but Mr. Case had not returned to the courtroom. The court waited until three o'clock when word came that Mr. Case was sick and would be unable to go on with the case that day. I asked that it be put over but the court insisted I should go on with the case. I asked the witness but a question or two and let him go. The state closed its case.

I thought the best way to win was to take the stand, that we would establish by our evidence that the killing was accidental and that there was no guilt on the part of our client; that he was not guilty of any crime or that he was guilty of willful murder. When I made the statement the Prosecuting Attorney jumped to his feet and declared that the state accepted the challenge. I introduced the evidence for the defense, putting both the defendant and his wife on the stand. The court was displeased with the action of the Prosecutor in accepting the proposition I had submitted and showed it in his instructions to the jury, for he gave four separate instructions on manslaughter in the fourth degree, but in my presentation of the case to the jury I argued that it was murder in the first degree or nothing, and as there was no evidence of deliberation or premeditation they must acquit the defendant.

The Jury was out about one hour when it returned with a verdict

Racing: Indian Style

of Not Guilty. I went down to the home of Mr. Case and told him of the verdict. His first question was, "How did you do it?", and I told him that I let the dangerous witness alone on cross-examination and then of my position in opening statement in which I set out what the defense would show.

The papers contained big write-ups of the trial, and one of the reporters who had practiced law freely commented upon the fact that I had put the prosecution "in a hole" and kept them there. From that time on, in every murder case that came to the office, it was made known that I was to take part in the trial. After I dissolved partnership with Mr. Case and became County Attorney I tried all murder and other criminal cases myself.

There were many interesting events that came up during the time I was at the bar. One of the most interesting happened in a Justice court. Our firm was retained to bring suit to recover damages because a team of horses, sold to our client, were unsound. I had been a race rider and had handled horses for years and in the trial of the case my experience came in good play. When the trial ended with a judgement for our client there were many comments on the case. One of the defendants said, "Young Curtis is not a lawyer, he is just a good horse man and knows more about horses than the law." Another said I should give up the law and become a veterinary surgeon.

My success in this horse case caused me to be retained in a number of cases growing out of horse deals. The most successful one was in 1882. I had often read of lawyers getting business from big men by their manner of conducting a lawsuit which they had won and I was greatly surprised one morning to be called into the Citizens Bank by Jonathan Thomas. I had been the attorney against him and had easily won the case; in fact, I won it on a demur to the evidence introduced by his attorney. He complimented me on having won the case and said he thought well of a lawyer who could win a lawsuit on the evidence introduced by the other side and that he would like to retain me as a lawyer for his bank and his several lumber companies. We entered into an agreement and I was his attorney from that time until I was elected to Congress, a period of about eleven years. I had many cases for him and won all of them.

One of the most interesting cases I ever had was when I was

defending a number of Gypsies who were charged with stealing a coon. They had the coon, and unexplained possession of property recently stolen is dangerous for those charged with having stolen the same. The Gypsies had a camp near the place from where the coon was stolen, they had been there for weeks; the men trading horses, the women telling fortunes, dancing and singing to entertain visitors.

The trial attracted a big crowd. When the state closed the case, I moved to discharge the defendants on the ground that a coon was a wild animal and, therefore, not subject to larceny. The Justice agreed with me and the defendants were discharged.

The Gypsies insisted that I should go to their camp with them, this I did and I was wonderfully treated. Every woman, young and old, insisted on telling my fortune. They entertained me with their songs, music and dances. For years after that trial the Gypsies who came to Topeka always looked me up and I was employed in a number of cases after that where the Gypsies were defendants.

We had a character, James Blue, practicing in the Justice Courts. He could not read but he could write his own name. He had been a Justice of the Peace in one of the states by reason of which was entitled to and was admitted to practice in lower courts of the state. This certificate entitled to admission in the Kansas bar. He was admitted but his practice was confined to the Justice courts in North Topeka and Soldier Township.

He was quite glib of tongue, spent nearly all his time around the saloons and was a leader among the elements that hang around such places. He always helped elect the Justices of the Peace in his ward and always demanded a jury in the cases he helped to try; this added to the costs and as the juries in the Justice courts were selected from the bystanders, he always had a friendly court and a jury made up of the men with whom he associated daily and it is said he generally won his cases.

One day he brought a suit against one of our clients, under a law that had been repealed by the last Legislature, but neither Jim nor the Justice knew that the law had been repealed. We told our client that we did not care to go before the Justice and suggested that he get another lawyer but he insisted that as we were his regular attorneys that we should represent him.

When a law is enacted by the Legislature of Kansas, the act usually provides when it shall take effect, and the date is generally fixed at the date of its approval by the Governor, the publication in the official State paper or its publication in the session laws. It was then customary for Crane and Company to print a paper covered volume giving the laws and the dates they would become effective.

I filed a motion to dismiss Mr. Blue's bill of particulars on the ground that the acts complained of had occurred since the repeal of the Statute under which the action was brought. We argued it pro and con but I shall never forget Jim Blue's argument. He paid his respects to "students of the law, prigs of the bar who were taken into big firms and were sent out to try cases in courts where the big lawyers of the firms considered themselves too big to appear," and he closed with the statement that the book I had brought into court did not contain the laws enacted by the Legislature; that it was unreliable and had likely been gotten up by the big lawyers to fool the Justice of the Peace. He picked up a copy of the Revised Statutes, lifted it above his head and said, "Look at this book containing the laws of the state, it is bound in sheep and the law is always bound in sheep," and slamming the book down on the table dramatically disclosed that, "His honor must not be fooled by a paper backed thing brought in by a prig of the bar."

The crowd seemed to be with him. I soon found the Justice of the Peace felt the same way. It took me some time to induce him to confer with the County Attorney to see who was right. He did this and the next morning he entered an order dismissing the case.

I could relate more about Jim Blue but the above gives an idea of the man and his influence with a pick up jury. When the saloons were closed and the joints disappeared, Jim Blue's success before juries was not nearly so great and he left Topeka and said he was going to a place where he could enjoy his personal liberty.

We had a deputy sheriff who had had years of experience in handling men charged with crime. One day during my term of office as the County Attorney, I caused the arrest of a man for selling whiskey. As soon as he was placed under arrest he began to act queer and those around the jail said he was crazy. The sheriff was convinced that he was and so were the others and men came to me and asked me if I were going to prosecute an insane man and they about convinced me he was insane, but I thought it best to send for the old deputy.

Charles Curtis

I told him what the people were saying and he replied that the man was not insane; that he was feigning and he asked me if I objected to his testing him. I did not know what he would do and I told him I had no objection. In about an hour he brought the man to my office. He was ready to talk, wanted to plead guilty to one count and promised when his time was up he would leave the county. I found that the deputy sheriff had simply turned the hose on him and threatened to keep the hose going as long as the man acted queer.

Under the prohibitory liquor law of Kansas, when first enacted, druggists who held permits could sell liquors for medicinal, mechanical and scientific purposes. The applicant was required to file an application under oath in which he set out the cause for which the liquor was desired. This application was to be filed with the Probate Court once a month and it was the duty of the County Attorney to go over them from time to time.

If one could print those old applications they would be more than interesting reading and ailments would appear to have been of many varieties. One day in looking over the list I found a man had purchased five gallons of whiskey and the ailment was plainly written "haying". The man was really putting up hay and wanted the stuff for his men, but the medical authorities did not note haying as a disability that called for liquor as a medicine, so the druggist paid a fine, lost his permit and closed his business.

After the saloons were closed, the joints driven out of business and the bootleggers were on the run, many complaints came in that men were getting something that had a "kick in it" and the police could not locate the place. Under the law, I had a right to subpoena witnesses; this I did and found that the men were going outside the city limits for whatever they were getting and after a day or two witnesses testified that they had bought cider from a certain man who was a very warm friend of mine and also of the other county officers. They testified that what they drank made them very drunk. I got out a warrant and a seizure order and the sheriff arrested the farmer and took charge of all his cider.

The old man insisted on seeing me before giving a bond. When they brought him to the office he was very indignant; wanted to know if there were any laws against his having an orchard and producing apples; if there were any laws against his making cider. I told him there was not, but he could not lawfully sell the cider if it were intoxicating and I told him from the evidence I had taken that his cider was giving satisfaction to those who desired to go on a "jag" and I asked him what he put in the cider that gave it a mule kick and he said, "Why, I put a double hand full of wheat, two quarts of raisins, and twenty-five pounds of raw lean meat in every barrel." This told the story and explained the many drunks that had been seen recently.

The sheriff opened one of the barrels; the wheat grains and the raisins were swollen and bursting open and the meat was about eaten up. The old man pled guilty, paid his fine and agreed to never again make cider for the market, and I don't think he ever did.

For a time, we had trouble with dives and joints; seemed to be unable to secure evidence promptly and when secured and the papers issued the officers would arrive on the scene too late, the offenders had apparently been tipped off. I thought the best way to end that was to get after the police who had been of but little assistance in the enforcement so we kept track of the policemen on the beats where the joints seemed to be operating and, in a day or two the reports came back in that a certain policeman by the name of John Stone had been seen in two or three joints. I sent for him and asked him to tell me of joints within his beat and asked him to file a complaint; this he refused to do.

Within two hours I had him under arrest, under the provisions of the law which fixed a penalty for officers who knew of violations of the law and neglected to report them to the county attorney. I also gave notice that I would arrest and prosecute every policeman who was guilty of such misconduct. The next morning a number of policemen called and made complaints and in a few days the joints were closed.

I kept the case against Stone pending as a warning and one day he notified me he would resign from the force and expected to leave the city and would do so if I could dismiss the case against him. I told him if he would resign and leave the city, that after he had been out of the city for six months, I would dismiss the case. He did resign and left the city and I dismissed the case. The bringing of this case did a lot of good as the other policemen were afraid of being arrested for non-performance of their duties.

Charles Curtis

One day reports came to the office that men were being arrested for being drunk but as a matter of fact they acted like crazy men. They swore they had purchased neither beer nor whiskey. I told the Chief of Police that when they were in proper condition to turn them loose with the instruction to report to the court the next morning. Soon after they were let out they were joined by plain clothes men, whom they did not know were such, and it was not long until they went to a cider stand which was located on the Avenue, there they bought a glass of sweet cider, but they asked for some pepper sauce and a bottle was handed them and they each put about a tablespoon full or two of pepper sauce in their glass of cider. They visited another stand, and then another, and at every stand visited cider was purchased and the pepper sauce was added.

After about the fourth stand had been visited the men were crazy drunk and so was one of the plainclothesmen. Warrants were issued for all the cider joints and they were put out of business and the "pepper sauce" souse was a thing of the past.

After the saloons were closed, clubs were formed and they gave a lot of trouble because the court had held it was not an offense for one man who had liquor to give it to another. The clubs became so bold and so open in their use of liquor that I thought it my duty to prosecute them and so I filed informations against two of the biggest clubs in the city. The Attorneys for the defendants were so sure they could win that they entered into an agreed statement of facts. The lower court found them guilty on the statement. They went to the Supreme Court and the highest court in the state sustained the District Court and affirmed the judgement of the lower court.

The Governor granted a pardon to the officers of one of the clubs against whom I had secured a conviction and that pardon gave a lot of trouble when it came to prosecuting clubs but I kept prosecution going whenever I heard of a club that was violating the law.

One day I was notified that big dealers intended to sell intoxicating liquors in the original packages. They opened up and displayed their goods, but they wanted me as County Attorney to agree to file an information, make a test case and let them run while the case was pending in the District and Supreme Courts. I refused to grant their request and

Racing: Indian Style

notified them I would arrest them on every sale made, for which I could secure evidence. They closed the place and returned the original packages to the state from which they had been shipped. Had I given my consent to stand on one case and make no more arrests, the operators would have had a fine opening for the liquor was done up in all size packages, from the smallest drink to a one-gallon jug, but I did not intend to give them a chance.

One day I heard that one of the clubs had brought in a carload of beer and several barrels of whiskey. I got out seizure papers for the liquor and soon had it in the possession of the Sheriff and at the trial I got an order for its destruction. He took it out back of the Court House where there was a hay yard and knocked the heads out of the kegs and barrels and let the stuff run out on the ground and through the hay. One of the deputies called me to the window and said, "See the fellows eating hay." There had quite a crowd gathered to witness the proceedings and some did have straws in their mouths and hands.

In looking over the returns of the druggists one month my attention was called to the fact that one druggist, whose place of business was adjoining one of the largest hotels in the city, had returned just two hundred sales for every day of the month. This caused me to look up his returns for several months back and I found just two hundred sales a day reported. I told the Probate Judge what I had found. He had charge of the issuance of the permits to the druggists and was custodian of their returns and received a small fee for every sale he returned. I told him I thought his friend - he had commended the druggist very highly - was violating the law. The Judge was sure that he was not. He asked me not to file a complaint until I had further evidence.

The next month I examined the returns of the druggist very carefully. You may judge my surprise when I found he had returned three hundred sales for every day of the month after the day I talked to the Probate Judge. I found a number of sales upon which I thought I could secure conviction and I knew the monthly returns would help me in the prosecution of the case.

I filed an information against the druggist and when the case came up for trial, his lawyers fought as hard as they could. When they put the defendant on the stand I questioned him about the returns and asked him how it happened that he returned just two hundred sales a day for months and then in one day the number had been increased to three hundred sales a day and had continued at that number ever since.

He said the Probate Judge had told him of my complaint about his returns and that he thought the Probate Judge wanted him to increase the number of returns because he, the Probate Judge, received five cents for each return. Those in the courtroom had a good laugh at the expense of the judge and he was about the maddest man I had ever seen.

Article No. X

While Prosecuting Attorney of Shawnee County, I took but few cases outside the county. There was one murder case in Republic County, the trial of which is referred to in the following clipping:

February 7, 1886.
Topeka Daily Capitol
COMPLEMENTARY TO OUR COUNTY ATTORNEY

We notice in one of our exchanges, the Belleville, Republic County, TELESCOPE, the following highly complementary notice of County Attorney, Charles Curtis, who returned last week from Belleville, where he was engaged in the prosecution of L. T. Hendrix, who murdered V. W. Kennedy, September 21, 1885.

Since Mr. Curtis returned from Belleville the jury in the case returned a verdict of guilty of manslaughter in the first degree. From the following notice we judge the Mr. Curtis acquitted himself in his customary creditable manner. "We had the pleasure last week of making the acquaintance of Honorable Charles Curtis, County Attorney of Shawnee County, who was here at the request of the family of Vallance W. Kennedy, to assist in the trial of Hendrix. Mr. Curtis is a man not over 26 years of age, and his face shows slight traces of Indian blood, but he is said to be one of the most popular County Attorneys that Shawnee has ever had. His argument of the case was able, eloquent and fair. No omissions of the other counsel escaped his notice, and he was quick to see an advantage and use it, but in a fair, honest and able manner. He talked for about an hour and a half, and often displayed a power of eloquence rarely equaled by so young a man. As he related the circumstance of the brutal and inexcusable murder, he dwelt upon the fact that had Kennedy been other than an Indian half-breed, his murderer would have thought twice before he killed him. His allusion to his people, the Indians, driven by the relentless white man from the Atlantic to the far west, driven only until the scattered remnants of once powerful nations remain, brought tears, and in any other place than a courtroom would have brought cheers from an appreciative audience."

I was re-elected County Attorney in November, 1886, for the term of two years from January 1887 - my majority was 1800. In that campaign the conditions were reversed. Some of the men who had been most active for me were opposing me, and those who fought me the hardest in 1884 were the most active supporters I had in 1886. This was because I had enforced the law, closed the saloons and kept them closed and I had prosecuted all law violators alike. We had a lot of fun in the campaign. They called our ticket "the dude ticket" because we were all young fellows, and those who wanted to defeat us got out a ticket of older men.

In going to one of our first meetings, we stopped at Auburn for our supper. W. E. Stearne was a candidate for Clerk of the District Court. After supper we were ready to start when we missed Mr. Stearne. I went into the house and found him in the kitchen explaining a cook book which he had just given to Mrs. Cozine, the good old woman who had gotten up our supper. When Stearne got into the wagon I told the boys what he was doing and we poked fun at him until he admitted he had a number of cook books under the seat and as we crossed the creek he dumped them all into the stream.

We told him that he would lose two votes. Mr. Cozine and the son-in-law would surely vote against him. He was greatly worried. A few days later when we were billed for the meeting about ten miles from Auburn, he insisted we should start early and go by Auburn and get our supper at Cozines. We arrived a little late; their regular supper was over and we had to take the leavings. The coffee was warmed over but Mr. Stearne took a second helping. The pie was cold and at least two days old and William asked for a second piece and he told Mrs. Cozine that the coffee and pie reminded him of the coffee and pie his mother made when he was a boy. We had great fun with him on the trip and when the votes came in from Auburn he was two votes behind the others on the ticket and we insisted that the cookbook had lost him two votes.

Those who opposed me had a letter printed advising the resubmissionists to vote against me because I had enforced the law against the saloon men and drug stores; in this letter they stated that the saloon men had elected me in 1884 and that I had gone back on them and had closed their places and driven them out of the state. One of my friends gave me a copy of the letter and I had a few of them struck off and saw that they reached some of the leading prohibitionists of the county so their little plan was used against them.

In driving out to a meeting one afternoon we passed a man who was having a time driving his cattle in a corral; one of the boys called out to him that he had a fine bunch of steers; he was hot all over and replied that they looked "damn good to the dudes just before election".

The following is an account of one of the murder cases I tried:

GUILTY
THE JURY CONVICTS JONES OF MURDER IN THE FIRST DEGREE. THE PRISONER UNCONCERNED BY THE AWFUL VERDICT RENDERED AGAINST HIM. MR. CURTIS' CLOSING SPEECH.

The defense made a motion for a new trial.

The district court met the eighth day of the trial of J. W. Jones at 9 o'clock yesterday morning. County Attorney Charles Curtis commenced the closing argument for the prosecution. In his speech to the jury which was one of great brilliancy and shrewdness, he made a great stride forward in his profession. His masterly effort of yesterday places him in the front rank of the rising young lawyers of the state, and establishes without a doubt his reputation as an untiring and successful prosecutor. In conducting the case he has shown no malice, but has discharged his duty to the state in a fearless and able manner. The result of the trial should be for him a cause for congratulation. It certainly reflects great credit upon him, all the more so because one of the counsel for the defense, Honorable A. H. Vance, one of the most eloquent advocates in the state, was pitted against him.

Charles Curtis

The following clippings show the feeling on the question of the County Attorney in 1888:

Topeka Capitol

March 24, 1888.

There is considerable talk as to who will be the nominees for the county offices this year. There is a County Attorney to elect, a clerk of the court, a probate judge and a county superintendent. Mr. Curtis is being asked to allow his name to be used for a third time for office of County Attorney but has not yet stated whether he will be a candidate or not. Among others who are being mentioned as candidates for this office are, J. C. Wood, W. B. Welch, J. S. Enstminger, and W. A. S. Bird. It seems quite probable that there will be no opposition to Judge Quinton and Clerk Sterne. They having served only one term. County Superintendent Mac-Donald has announced that he will not be a candidate for renomination. So far as known there are three gentlemen who would like to be his successor, vis: Josiah Jordan, E. C. Shull, and J. M. Howard.

News

March 24, 1888.

Of a half dozen persons so far named for the next county attorney the News does not hesitate to declare in favor of the present incumbent.

Courier

March 25, 1888.

The News is in favor of Charles Curtis for County Attorney. Mr. Curtis could be re-elected without the aid of that paper if he would accept the office again.

March 31, 1888.

The Topeka newspaper fellows are booming Charles Curtis for a third term as County Attorney. St. Mary's Gazette. Correct, Brother Carpenter, we know a good thing when we see it.

Racing: Indian Style
Mail and Breese, Topeka
July 23, 1888.

Charles Curtis was renominated by acclamation for the office of County Attorney. So well and faithfully has he performed his duties that there was no opposition to him. Charles Curtis has proven himself one of the most efficient officers the county has ever had. In the face of the strongest opposition he has effect fully enforced all laws. Few men of his years have such force and magnetism in their makeup. Whenever he says anything people know he means it. Whenever he makes a pledge people have found out that he fulfills it. He is a terror to all evil doers and a young man of whom Shawnee should be proud.

News
May 15, 1888.

It is said that Mr. Curtis will not again be a candidate for County Attorney. This, if true, is a judicious course for him. While true if a candidate he might readily succeed, he can now retire with better prestige and with better chances for the future than if he used his present popularity to secure renomination. He has made a most creditable record.

TOPEKA DAILY CAPITOL
July term, 1888.
In the Courts.

The criminal docket for the present term of the district court was finished yesterday with the sentence of the prisoners convicted of various offenses. Southworth, Holmes and Stark were sentenced. Southworth getting six years for Grand larceny, Holmes two years for participating in the same offense, and Stark sentenced for an assault with intent to commit murder. The record of the Court during this term has been such as to insure protection to the community - protection against crime, and to indicate to the criminal class that for offenses in this county, punishment will be swift and certain. The County Attorney, Charles Curtis, has the satisfaction of securing conviction in every case tried before the court, and by his ability, faithfulness and industry, continuing his record as public prosecutor, which is second to none in the state.

Charles Curtis

The following is the comments of the Capitol on the trial of a case in the District Court:

It was thought by a great many that Mr. Waters had covered the ground in the case so completely that there would be nothing for Mr. Curtis to say. But the court and bar pronounced his address and review of the evidence very complete indeed. It was considered one of the finest and most able speeches ever made in Shawnee County. The jury in the case is composed of the most prominent and substantial men in the county. The rulings of the court throughout the entire case have been commented upon as being very able and impartial. The rulings in this case have proved Judge Guthrie to be a very able jurist. The case will go to the jury at 9 A. M. today.

In 1888, I offered my services as a speaker to the Republican State Central Committee. I was given a try out at Phillipsburg. The following is a copy of the letter sent to the State Organization by the County Organization of Phillips County. This letter was written after my meeting there and without my knowledge.

Phillipsburg, Kansas.
September 17, '88.

Republican State Central Committee,
    Topeka, Kansas.

Gents:

Since our meeting here on Saturday I have intended to write you but have been very busy - Our meetings were a grand success - Mr. Felt made one of his stirring and pleasing talks to a house as crowded as could be and all were pleased and at the same time remarks by leading men were current to the effect that whilst Mr. Humphrey was not an easy talker his very appearance was an assurance of ability and honesty.

In the evening we again had equally as crowded a house and the young man, Charles Curtis, made a speech that is hard to beat. He dealt largely in figures and convincing argument. He is a very able speaker and took well. In fact, it is a common remark by leading public men here that Felt made a good talk but Curtis a better one.

I wish in justice to Mr. Curtis & in the interest of the party to urge you upon that you use this man all you can - his talks win votes.

Yours very truly,
(signed) George Spaulding.

The speech at Phillipsburg marked my entrance in state politics in Kansas and upon my return home I was requested to call at State Headquarters and was shown the letter and asked if I would like to fill the appointments of Honorable Thomas Ryan, the then Congressman from that District, and the Republican nominee for re-election. I gladly accepted the assignments and was at once started out to fill dates which had already been fixed and meetings advertised in the name of Congressman Ryan.

That campaign was the beginning of my acquaintance with the people of the Fourth District, as I was a stranger in all the counties except Shawnee, my home, and Osage and Wabaunsee Counties where I had frequently attended Court.

I had good meetings and made a large number of friends, many of whom, I am pleased to say, have remained my warm friends and active supporters ever since.

Excerpt from Article No. XII

Many members of the Farmers Alliance of 1889 had helped organize the Populist Party, which in the year had become a strong political factor. It was apparent that they would carry the Fourth Congressional District for John G. Otis, a milk man of Topeka. They did more. They carried the State Legislature and elected William A. Peffer to the Senate to succeed John J. Ingalls. They elected five out of the seven Congressmen. Among others Jerry Simpson (known as sockless Jerry) of Medicine Lodge, defeated W. L. Hallowell (known as Prince Hall) of Wichita, Kansas. The Republicans elected Honorable Case Broderick of the First District and Honorable E. H. Funston (father of General Fred Funston) from the Second District. The Populists carried the Fourth District by nearly five thousand majority.

That campaign brought to the front Jerry Simpson, Ben Clover, John Davis, William Baker, John G. Otis, Jeff Hudson, William A. Peffer, Mrs. Diggs, Mary Ellen Lease and many other Populist leaders. Of them all, I believe Mrs. Lease was the strongest on the stump. She did the Republicans more harm than any other one campaigner sent out by the Populist organization. She carried her crowds wherever she spoke and was busy day and night. Mrs. Diggs was very strong but not quite as effective as Mrs. Lease.

A story of the rise and fall of the Populist Party would be interesting and I hope someday someone who was a member of that organization may tell the people of Kansas all about it. They differed from the dissatisfied elements of today in this - they had their own organization and fought under their own political banner. They drew from both political parties. In all combinations they forced recognition of their organization. They made a wonderful showing in Kansas in 1890 and 1892.

In 1888, Benjamin Harrison, as the Republican candidate for President, carried Kansas by nearly ninety thousand. All the Congressional Districts went Republican. But in 1890, the Populists' carried six of the then eight Congressional Districts. They had a majority on a joint ballot of the State Legislature. And in January 1891, they defeated Honorable John J. Ingalls for re-election to the Senate with William A. Peffer.

In Washington they tell a good story about Ingalls and Peffer. They say that in the fall of 1889 Peffer came to Washington at the head of a delegation representing the Farmers Alliance of Kansas. Their object was to secure legislation desired by the farmers of the central west. Among others, they desired to consult Senator Ingalls. They sent word to him that Mr. Peffer of Topeka, Kansas, and a delegation from that state representing the Farmers Alliance desired to see him. Mr. Ingalls, instead of giving them a date, asked, "who was this man Peffer?"

When the news was returned to Peffer it is said he replied that they would go back to Kansas and show Senator Ingalls who this man Peffer really was. Upon his return to the state he began the organization of the Populist Party. He was their first candidate for the United States Senate and was elected.

Politically, 1890 was a great year for me.

I went to one of the Populist picnics to hear Mrs. Lease and get her line of argument. She was a wonder and I shall never forget that meeting. It was held in a grove just outside the city limits of Rossville. I was the guest of the Bond families; John and William. He had a lunch on the grounds - fried chicken, pickled beets, cucumber pickles, bread, cakes, pies, jellies and preserves of all kinds. In short, just the kind of a lunch the good farmers' wives would prepare for such an occasion.

While eating, one of the brothers said he had sold his hogs, cattle and corn and had the money (several thousand dollars) in the bank. He asked my advice as to investing it. I told him to buy more Kaw bottom land or put it in good first mortgage loans; the other brother said he had a lot of hogs and cattle and plenty of corn and he was uncertain what to do. I told him Grandfather Curtis always advised holding cattle and hogs when they and corn were both low in the market.

We had barely finished our lunch before Mrs. Lease was introduced. She was tall and the boys said, "raw-boned" but when she began to talk, one forgot her looks and she had not been talking long until she had most of the crowd leaning over in their anxiety to hear what she was saying.

It was not long before I missed one of the Bond brothers. I looked around in an effort to locate him and mentioned to the brother the fact that I did not see him. In a few minutes we located him. He had moved up in front and was standing just a few feet from the speaker and was taking in every word she was saying. It was not long before the other brother got up and joined the crowd standing near the speaker. When the speech was over the crowd gathered around Mrs. Lease. It was sometime before she could get away.

Had it not been for one mistake she made, I think she would have captured all of her hearers. She referred in uncomplimentary terms to the General Logan family, and said the grandson, a mere child, had been made an officer in the Illinois State Militia and that he was drawing an officer's salary. This did not take well with the ex-Union soldiers for they all loved and admired General John A. Logan, and I could see that many of the veterans of the Civil War did not go up to shake her hand.

When the Bond brothers came back they both began to talk at once and said she was right and etc. I told them of our conversation at lunch - about the money the one had in the bank and didn't know what to do with it and of the cattle, hogs and corn the other still had but it did no good. They were for Mrs. Lease and the Populist doctrines.

I told them that I remembered when they left North Topeka for their farms above Rossville; how hard up they were then and what fine farms they now owned and how well off they had become and that they had made it all off their farms but it did no good. I think the best illustration as to the power and growth of the Populist party was shown in Rossville Township.

The report came down to Topeka on election day that the Populists had formed in companies and that there was one man in charge of every ten and that they marched through a doctor's office for their tickets and then in squads of ten marched to a voting place and put in their ballots. No one was permitted to approach them. The Captain saw to that.

One of the things that made the Populist party strong in 1890 was that they took their women folks in to their organizations and they held many meetings behind closed doors where they talked of the sub-treasury and the fiat money plans and other doctrines they advocated. Then early in the campaign of 1890, they refused to go out to the meetings of the Republicans but before the campaign was over they were all loaded with what they had read in Colonel Harvey's Financial School and many of them went out to ask questions. One had to be posted or the Populist in the audience would ask questions and would down them with the questions asked. I remember I bought a copy of Colonel Harvey's book and studied it and all the questions raised in it and I had a lot of fun in that campaign. I was posted on both sides.

I remember a meeting at Waverly, Kansas. The first speaker, Judge Garver, did not try to answer the questions asked and the crowd got restless and excited. I had hardly been introduced before men in the audience began asking questions. I had a ready answer for them all and soon had them all quieted but one old fellow. At last, I made up my mind from the questions asked and the way the crowd took my answer to his questions, that he was not a farmer but that he must be a money loaner or had been, so, I concluded to take a shot at him and between questions I told the audience that the trouble did not come from the farmer but was brought about by the class of men who loaned them small amounts at 2% a month and took a cut-throat mortgage on all the personal property on the place and if payments were not promptly made they took the property and I judged from the questions asked by the gentleman that he belonged to that class. The crowd went wild for a few minutes and many yelled, "Hit him again, he is old two percent all right." I had no more trouble with questions. Our meeting lasted until after one o'clock that night. I don't think a single person left the building. They were having too much fun.

I attended one meeting that did not last long. It was not because of questions asked but because of the free use of rotten vegetables. It seems that Governor Humphrey had been advertised to speak at Scranton, Osage County. The local candidates had held a meeting there about

Racing: Indian Style

one week before the Governor's date. This meeting was broken up and notice was served that if the Republicans attempted to hold another meeting there that they would not be permitted to do so. The friends of the Governor, having heard of what had happened at the first meeting, thought it best not to send him down so the State Committee wired me to come in to fill that date.

When I arrived in Topeka, I was not told of the trouble at Scranton but was advised to go down to Burlingame on an early train and drive back to Scranton for the meeting. Mr. Brown, the Mayor of Concordia, Kansas, a Republican spellbinder, happened to be at headquarters and had nothing on for the night and said he would like to go with me. We got our lunch, went to Burlingame on the early afternoon train and called upon Charles Sheldon, the Republican Chairman for that county.

He asked us what we were doing down in Osage County and I told him we had been sent down to take the place of Governor Humphrey at Scranton and asked him to get some of the boys to go down with us. He said he would not go to a meeting at Scranton for a hundred dollars. He told us of the county meeting and what was in store for us. He thought the meeting had better be called off as they would not permit us to hold it, but I insisted that I was not afraid and Brown drove to Scranton.

We arrived a little early, went to the hotel and registered; then started out to find the County Committeeman. He was not at his place of business and we were told that he would not be back for the meeting. We then asked to be directed to some Republican. The party with whom we were talking said there were but few in the town.

We called upon Dr. Packer who was a Republican and not afraid to say so but he doubted the wisdom of having a meeting. We went back to the hotel and had our supper and in a little while two or three men came to the hotel to talk about the meeting. We told them we were there and willing to take a chance, then the question came up as to who should preside. No one was anxious for the honor. At last, one of them said he would call the meeting to order but he would not go upon the stage. I asked him why and he said he was afraid some parties intended to throw ripe vegetables at the Chairman and speakers.

I supposed they would try to break up the meeting by asking questions but I had no idea that they would resort to throwing decayed vegetables at us. We were asked which would talk first and Brown insisted that I should as I had been sent down to take the place of the Governor. The crowd was on hand at 7:30, the hall was jammed. The man who had promised to introduce us stood down in front and announced the fact that the Governor could not be with them but that Charles Curtis of Topeka and Mr. Brown of Concordia would talk to them on the issues of the day. Brown and I were on the platform or stage. I had hardly begun my speech before a tomato thrown from the outside and through a side door went whizzing by. I stepped back out of range of a door and went on. The audience gave me the silent treatment. No story I told brought a laugh and nothing I said was applauded and a time or two I stepped in range of the door or a window which opened on the stage and a tomato or potato was thrown at me. It was hard work.

I tried talking the old flag and patriotism but there was no response. At last, I told a story that had not failed to bring down the house, where ever told, but the result was the same except an old man who seemed to be drunk got up and said he would like to ask me a question, and I told him I would be pleased to have him do so. He said, "Well, I hearn that story afore."

They crowd seemed to be delighted with this exposure of my old story and showed it by laughing and applauding. I talked a while longer and wound up with a story and ended by saying, "Perhaps my drunken friend in the center aisle has hearn that story afore," and sat down. The audience applauded.

I never knew whether it was because I quit talking or because of my fling at the old man. I had just been talking thirty minutes, while I usually talked fifty or sixty minutes, and if questions were asked an hour and a half.

When I sat down, Mr. Brown got up, rolled up his sleeves and asked, "Do you know who I am?" Someone came back with, "We don't care but tell us." Brown said, "I am the fighting Mayor of Concordia. I am the Mayor who licked a man on the streets of that city the other day." Someone in the audience came back with, "He must have been a damn small man," and the crowd yelled. Brown was a little excited and stepped to the front of the stage and whack came a potato and hit him broadside; he stepped back and talked on for a few minutes when another vegetable was thrown in.

It missed him but he stepped out of range again and began to

Racing: Indian Style

talk and perspire. I never saw *(a)* man use his handkerchief so often as he did in so short a time. In a few minutes, he stopped. We both had occupied less than an hour. When we got through the crowd didn't go out as they usually did but many stayed and said they didn't want to hear us talk politics but would like to visit with us and we put in a very interesting and pleasant hour until train time. Just before we left the crowd said they hoped we would come again and that if we would that they would assure us there would be no disturbance. A number went down to the depot with us. Two years later I had one of the best meetings of the campaign at Scranton.

Excerpt from Article No. XIII

I had a number of interesting experiences in the campaign of 1890. At many of the meetings, questions were asked, this made them interesting and gave the audience some excitement and the speaker always had the best of it. It was the cold silent crowds that got you.

I will never forget my meeting at Rosalia, among the flint hills in Butler County. I arrived with no one at the train. I went up to the post office but the Postmaster ran the largest general store in the little town and I could see at once that he was afraid to take any part in a meeting and really disliked to be seen with anyone connected with the Republican party, although he was holding the office as an appointee under President Harrison.

He told me that there were only seventeen Republicans in the township and that he was the only one in the town and that the hotel had been closed the day before; that all but the seventeen in the township were active Populists except a very ***(few)*** Democrats and he thought they would vote the Populist ticket. He said he did not have time to introduce me to people of the town (it would not have taken him long) so I left him in disgust.

As I left his store a man with a Grand Army button in the lapel of his coat went by and I said, "You are the man I am looking for," he replied, "I do not know whether I am or not, you are the young Curtis who is to speak here tonight, why don't you go to your Republican postmaster?" I said, "I had called upon him and I thought he had a big streak of yellow." He then told me that his name was Smith and if I would go over to his house he would have my name put in the pot for dinner and supper and promised I should not miss the morning train for El Dorado.

I went with him and was introduced to his wife and then I began to urge Mr. Smith to preside at the meeting. He insisted there were so few Republicans in the township that there was no use having a meeting but, he said, "If you do have one this old hall will be full and there won't be a baker's dozen of Republicans there and the Postmaster won't be there."

After considerable urging he said he would not preside at the meeting but that he would call the meeting to order, introduce me and then take his seat in the crowd, but he would do that only upon the condition that I promise that if we carried the election, I would recommend the removal of the Postmaster. I told him he need not ask for that promise for I had already made up my mind to write the Congressman and tell him all about the Postmaster and ask for his removal.

In a little while, a Mr. Tilden, the Republican candidate for the legislature from that district appeared at the door. Mr. Smith invited him in and we then went over the ground fully and I told him about the Postmaster. We both had dinner and supper with Mr. Smith and his wife and they were good meals.

In the afternoon and evening, he introduced us to the folks in town and those who came in town. The crowd gathered early and the hall was soon filled. As they entered the hall the women went to one side and the men to the other side. This was true of old and young alike. I do not remember of seeing a man on the side occupied by the women nor a woman on the side occupied by the men.

Mr. Smith kept his word and introduced me. Mr. Tilden said he would not talk. The crowd was silent and cold - no demonstration. I covered all the issues. We had been told to make special reference to Senator John J. Ingalls and when I referred to him, I thought I could see the audience getting colder. I then talked of the Union soldiers and the Civil War. When I referred to copperheads, an old man arose and asked me what I meant by copperheads and I described them as they had been described to me by those who knew them back in Indiana during the great Civil War and why I did it, I don't know, but I ended my description by saying, "Perhaps you were one of them?"

The words were hardly out of my mouth before shouts came from the various parts of the room, "You are right, hit him again." From then on, the audience responded to my speech in great shape.

Racing: Indian Style

When I concluded a dozen or more men and women came up to shake hands and thank me for my speech and the leader of the Populist organization asked me to announce for him that a car of coal was on the side track and that members of their organization needing coal could be supplied if they would call the next morning. This I did and nearly all the crowd seemed to leave the hall feeling fine.

Our ticket got a good vote in that township that fall and local candidates gave me credit for breaking the ice for them. They said from that meeting on to the end of the campaign, they had good meetings in that township.

THE KILLING OF SAM WOOD

Of the twenty-eight murders I tried, or assisted in the trial of, the prosecution of James Brennan for the killing of Sam Wood attracted the most attention in the newspapers, not because of the result of the trial or what happened at it, but because Sam Wood was one of the Kansas pioneers and had been one of the leading characters in Kansas for many years. He had belonged to the various political parties and at one time made the race as the candidate of the Greenback anti-monopoly and the Greenback labor parties for Congress and was defeated.

Judge Samuel R. Peters was elected and Sam Wood contested the election on the ground that Peters was a Judge of the District Court at the time of his election. He contended that under the Constitution of the State of Kansas that a District Judge could not hold any other office during the term for which he had been elected. This contention was not sustained by the House of Representatives. The report of the Committee was written by Honorable M. F. Elliott, then a Democratic member of the Congress and afterwards General Attorney for the Standard Oil Company.

As the early settlers will well remember, S. N. Wood was always active on one side or the other of every movement in Kansas, from his arrival in the fifties to his death in 1891. That he was cowardly and brutally murdered, no one who knows the facts will deny. That those who were responsible for his murder were never punished in the courts was because the protection of the laws threw around everyone charged with the crime. That is, the assurance of a trial by a jury in the county in which the crime was committed.

Charles Curtis

I was employed by the State to assist in the prosecution. It was supposed that the case which was called for trial November term of the District Court, 1891 at Hugoton, Kansas would be handled by Attorney General Ives, County Attorney William O'Connor and me, and the defendant was represented by J. N. Pitzer and J. D. Snoddy. The District Judge, because of certain charges as to his connection with the case, could not sit as trial judge, so it was agreed that Judge Wall of Wichita should act as Judge Pro Tem to try the case.

Early in November, 1891, Attorney General Ives and I left Topeka for Hugoton on the Rock Island. We were to go to Liberal on the train and take the stage from Liberal to Hugoton. I will never forget that trip. Some place between Herrington and Liberal we passed a lake. There were thousands of wild ducks in the lake and we all regretted we were not going hunting rather than to try a lawsuit.

We arrived in Liberal early in the evening. We had our suppers at the depot eating house and then struck out for Hugoton. At Liberal, our party was joined by Judge Wall and a mortgage adjuster.

Nearly every homestead we passed had been abandoned, the old sod houses had nearly all been removed and in one case, all the fixtures of a windmill had been taken away. I remember the adjuster insisted on getting out and examining the place. He said the company held a mortgage on it and he must see what was left. When he returned he said the house was gone, the horse and cow sheds were gone and the well had been pulled up and he thought the only thing on the place at that time was a few acres of tumbleweeds and the mortgage of his company. The comments of the adjuster were very amusing to us but we could tell what he saw of the places upon which his company had mortgages had made him sick.

We arrived in Hugoton late at night and found a real western or frontier hotel. We were all tired and went to bed at once. The next morning, I got up early. I had breakfast at the first table and then went out to see what I could see.

Hugoton was a typical short grass county seat town in a county where there had been a county seat fight from the day the county was organized. I had not been in front of the hotel very long when I saw two men coming down the street; one was a very large man and both men had Winchesters *(rifles)* on their shoulders. I asked a bystander who the man in front was and was told that he was Judge Botkin, and that the man behind him was a Mr. Short, a deputy U. S. Marshal, and a deputy sheriff, and a bodyguard of the Judge.

I followed the men who fell in behind the Judge to the building where the court was being held. The Judge walked up to the bench and laid his Winchester over it. Mr. Short walked up to the side of the Judge and stood by the bench with the butt of his Winchester resting on the floor.

The court was opened, quite an amount of business was transacted before the arrival of Judge Wall and Attorney General Ives. I watched with the greatest interest everything that happened. I had not been in the room long before I discovered that nearly every man in it, except myself, was armed. Big revolvers showed below their coats or bulged at their hips. Judge Wall and Attorney General Ives came into the courtroom about nine thirty a.m. and as soon as Judge Botkin disposed of some minor matters he called Judge Wall, who had been selected to try the Brennan case, to the bench and he and Short with their Winchesters left the room.

When the case came up the Attorney General announced that I had been called into the case by the state and that I would represent him in the case. Twelve jurors were called into the jury box and the work of selection of a jury to try the case of the State of Kansas vs. James Brennan began.

It soon appeared that the men on the south side were working to be kept on the jury. The friends of the late Sam Wood claimed they desired to be selected so they could acquit the defendant; it also appeared that the men drawn from the north side were doing everything possible to be selected and the friends of the defendant contended they were doing so because they hoped to convict the defendant. In short, it appeared to be a fight between the residents of the south side against the residents of the north side and I was doing my best to secure a jury that would give a fair and impartial trial.

I will never forget one Irishman who lived on the south side and made every effort to stay on the jury. I soon discovered his purpose and so asked him all manner of questions, but, at last I asked him the old standby question, "Have you expressed any opinion as to whether or not Sam Wood is dead?" He looked at me for a second and then said, "Is Sam Wood dead? Is Sam Wood dead? And bejabbers, didn't I brush the flies off him meself." When his answer was out I said I challenged the juror for cause and the Judge said, "Stand aside." The old Irishman said in a low voice as he passed me, "You think you are damn smart, don't you?"

I found that after it was announced that I was to represent the Attorney General in the trial of the case and had begun to question the men called in the jury box that I was being closely watched as was the Judge. At noon, the court took a recess until two o'clock. Several men followed us to the hotel. I went up to my room and had been there but a few moments when I heard a knock at the door.

I called, "Come in" and in a minute a man came who seemed very much excited. He said he lived across the street from the church where the killing of Sam Wood occurred; that he was at home that morning and saw all the movements of the various parties and he would tell me all and would testify to all on the stand, if I would guarantee him protection. This, I promised to do and he gave me all the facts and I made up my mind that more men than the defendant had helped arrange for the killing of Sam Wood, and I felt that the County Attorney would do everything he could to protect them and to assist the defendant, and that it would be well for me to pretend to know nothing but watch the County Attorney.

I went without my dinner in order to get the story of the man who called and I told the Attorney General Ives of my interview and asked him to take the afternoon hack for Liberal and when he reached there to get in touch with the Governor and have General Hoisington and a few state militiamen sent up and asked that they come in plain clothes. I also asked him to leave written authority for me to represent him.

It was well I did this because as soon as it was known that the Attorney General had left the city, the County Attorney began to try to control the case and at one point objected to my appearance in the case, as he had not asked the state for assistance. To save any further trouble, I filed with the court the letter of the Attorney General, and the court, who knew the situation, recognized my authority and so advised the County Attorney.

The attorneys for the defense, who had been backing the County Attorney and the jury asked that he not recognize me as being in charge of the prosecution. The County Attorney was very mad and left the courtroom but returned in a couple of hours and when the court adjourned he asked me to go to his office. I notified some of the men that I was going and they advised me not to do it, and suggested I disregard him. I went to his office. We gathered chairs around a big stove in the front room. I could see that he was mad. He asked me how I got into the case and I told him I supposed the state had employed me because of my experience in the trial of murder cases. He asked me if they had tried to involve him and I told him that Governor and the Attorney General had not referred to him in any way.

He wanted to know why I did not let him take the lead in the case and I told him frankly that as he had lived there during the contest and no doubt had been in the county seat fight that I thought it best for the prosecution to be conducted by one who had no prejudices and one who would seek to secure a jury that would give a fair trial. He asked me if I knew I was being watched by both sides. I told him I had noticed that I was followed wherever I went, but as I intended to do my duty and get out all the facts in the case that I did not care how much watching was done. He said, "You intend to bring out all the facts surrounding the killing of Sam Wood?" I told him I did.

I had hardly completed my statement until he was on his feet and talking loud about not having been given fair treatment and then turned to the stove and pointed to a big round hole in the stove pipe and then to a like hole in the board partition and said, "Do you see that bullet hole in that stovepipe and the one in that partition?" I told him that I did. He said, "Well, this faithful old gun of mine went off accidentally the other day and made those holes and it might go off accidentally again and kill a man."

I said with all the men out in the street I was not afraid of his gun going off accidentally or otherwise; that I intended to try the case in my own way and if he had any further communication he might submit the same in open court; that I happened to have been born in Kansas and that I was not afraid of guns nor of men who carried them and I bid him good day and walked out of his office.

When court met again he was not in the courtroom and I did not see him again until the next day. On Friday noon the sheriff came to me and told me if we were not careful there would be trouble the next day (Saturday); that he had scoured the county and was unable to find any more men for the jury. We had up to that time examined twenty-nine men, one minor and one who was so weak mentally that the court had to excuse him and had only secured seven jurors and each side still had several peremptory challenges left.

I told the court of the situation and also advised him of the fears of the sheriff, and in order to get the fighting factions out of town we agreed that I should announce that I had a motion which I wished to file and that as it was a matter for the court to pass upon, I suggested that the jurors and witnesses be discharged until the next Monday and that the court could take a recess until eight p.m. in order to give me time to draw my motion.

The attorneys for the defense strenuously objected and stated they wanted trial by jury and they regretted the case had not been sent to some other county for trial. I responded that if the defendant wanted a change of venue to another county that the state would consent but no such motion was filed by them and the court granted my request that the witnesses and jurors be discharged until Monday and for a recess until eight p.m. and admonished the jurors and witnesses as to their duties and said as they had been in attendance all the week he would dismiss them until the next Monday morning at nine o'clock.

During the recess, I drew a motion for a change of venue setting out fully the various statements that had been made by the attorneys for the defendant about being sorry that they could not have the case tried in a county where there would be no trouble in securing a fair and impartial jury and the anxiety of the defendant for a speedy trial and for those reasons and the fact that because of the notoriety of the case it was almost certain that it would be impossible to secure a jury.

When I presented the motion, I argued it at some length reviewing what had been said by the attorneys for the defendant and the answer of the men who had been called as jurors. The attorneys for the defendant were so taken by surprise that they seemed to have forgotten the constitutional provisions and the decisions of the court and were unable to do anything but bluster and talk loudly. After a little time, I asked to interrupt and stated that, of course, if the defendant would not consent that the State could not have a change of venue; that it was a matter wholly in the hands of the defendant and I cited the Court to the decision of the Supreme Court and told the court that in view of the attitude of the attorneys for the defendant there was but one thing for me to do and that was to withdraw my motion. I then told the court that the sheriff had a report to make.

The sheriff reported that he had brought into court every man eligible for jury service in the county and that it was impossible to secure any more. The court entered an order discharging the jury, dismissed the witnesses, continued the case until the next term of court and ordered the defendant to be held without bail and that he would be committed to Reno County Jail.

Racing: Indian Style

Our wagons were ready and we paid our hotel bills, packed our grips and started for Liberal. We had gone about ten miles when we were halted by a number of horsemen from the north part of the county. When they haled us, I told them what had happened; they said they had nothing against us, the Judge and I, and that they didn't have time to talk and that the sheriff would never get Brennan to Liberal. They struck out for the south.

It was early in the morning when we arrived at Liberal. We had our breakfast at the depot restaurant. We told the conductor what had happened and that the sheriff was expecting to reach Liberal with Brennan before the train pulled out. He agreed to hold the train for a short time.

Starting time passed, the conductor and passengers were impatient and it looked as though we would be unable to have the train held longer. When, on looking east, we saw a cloud of dust and soon the sheriff was in sight and the train was held until he drove up and got Brennan into one of the cars.

Brennan was held in jail the time required by law and then was released because it was impossible to get a jury in Stevens County to try him. He moved to Oklahoma after his release from jail and I understand he was re-arrested a number of years ago and taken back to Stevens County but that again it was found impossible to secure a jury and he was again discharged. He was never tried and all the facts in regard to the killing of Sam Wood were never made public. Had they been, I am sure that the people of Kansas would have been convinced beyond a doubt that he was deliberately killed in cold blood and that other men were accessories before the fact.

I always regretted that the old man who told me his story of the acts of certain parties just before the killing and what he saw of the shooting did not have an opportunity to tell the public what he had seen.

I have been told that James Brennan passed away a few years ago and that during the last few years of his life he was considered insane by those who lived near him. In this connection, it is interesting to read the last paragraph of the memorial of Samuel N. Wood written by his widow Margaret L. Wood.

The persons implicated in the murder of Colonel Wood cannot blot out the evidence against them and whether principal or accessories, the memo-

ry of that cruel deed will forever haunt them. An unseen presence will remind them of that deed of blood, and sometimes before their inner vision will pass a pale, blood stained face they will shudder to see. A Nemesis will follow them, and in the hereafter, from the depths of the hell they have made for themselves, they will implore S. N. Wood to forgive and help them.

There is plenty of time for retribution - all of this life, and the eternal years in addition. His widow and children and friends can wait.

"Though the mills of God grind slowly, yet they grind exceedingly small; Though with patience he stands waiting, with exactness grinds he all."

I visited Stevens County a few years ago and was told that before Mr. Brennan died that he went insane.

Article No. XIV

THE CLAIRVOYANT

One day a richly dressed and prosperous looking colored woman called at our office and going to the desk of Mr. Case said, "You are not the lawyer I am looking for but I know he is in this building. He is a young fellow, tall and slender and has black hair and eyes. I saw him while in a trance and he is the lawyer I am looking for."

Mr. Case told her she had better look in the other room and she might find the man she wanted. She came to the door and upon seeing me said, "That's the man." She came in and all she wanted was a divorce. After talking with her for a while I agreed to bring the suit for her, then she insisted on telling who she was and all about her business and how she was able to solve so many mysteries and tell so many people of their past, their present and their future.

In due time her divorce was granted but for years afterward men and women would come to my office and tell me they had been sent by Mrs. Johnson; the Clairvoyant. She did many things that attracted attention to her and brought her many callers who desired to have their fortune told or to locate mining property.

It is said that at one time two women called upon her; one had lost some jewelry and desired to be directed where she could find it. Mrs. Johnson, after going into a trance, told her if she would look in the purse of the friend who was with her she would find her missing jewelry and she did. The lady explained that she had taken the jewelry in fun, that she knew her friend would call upon Mrs. Johnson and that she wanted to test her powers.

A farmer missed a very valuable blooded calf and thought it had been stolen. He called upon Mrs. Johnson and after going into a trance, she told the man that his calf had not been stolen but that a neighbor had driven a herd of cattle by the pasture and that his calf had gotten out at a place where there was a loose wire in the fence and that if he would look at a bunch of cattle in a field a little beyond his place that he could find his calf, and the farmer followed her directions and found his calf. I could relate many more instances of the Clairvoyant's power but think these two enough to explain why Mrs. Johnson had so many callers.

That it pays a lawyer to carefully study his cases and be ready to meet any question that may come up has been realized many times by every practicing attorney. I remember having been retained to assist a lawyer in the defense of a number of men who were charged with using the United States Mails with the intent to defraud. I was confident the attorney whom I was to assist would not be fully prepared, so I took it upon myself to study the case from every angle. The trial came on and I was soon placed in full charge of the defense. I was ready on every question and made it quite interesting for the United States District Attorney and while one of the defendants was convicted, I succeeded in acquitting the other three.

In a few days, I began to receive letters from Kansas City, St. Louis, Chicago and other cities asking me to fix dates when they might see me and others were asking how much I would charge for a written opinion on various questions. This kept up as long as I was in active practice and I was employed to go to Des Moines, Iowa, to defend a number of men who had been arrested on a charge of using the mails to defraud. The employment came because a representative of the men had been a spectator at the trial in Topeka. I am relating this instance hoping it may encourage young lawyers to more carefully prepare the cases in which they may be called upon to try.

THE TESSON MURDER CASE

Louis Tesson, a Sioux and Fox Indian killed Henry Washburn, an Indian and a member of the same tribe. He was arrested in the state courts but when it developed that the killing was done on the Sioux and Fox Indian

Reservation, an order was issued to turn him over to the United States authorities, but before he could be delivered to the proper authorities, he made his escape and was away some six or seven years when he returned to the Reservation.

As an indictment had been returned against him in the United States District Court, he was arrested and I was employed to defend him. After I was retained for the defense I visited the Reservation for the purpose of going over the ground where the killing had occurred and to talk with the witnesses. I found there had been an afternoon and night party and that during the late evening, the two men had quarreled and that Tesson had left the party - gone to his home, secured his revolver, painted his face and put his bear claws around his neck and then returned to the party. He had been back but a few minutes when he was accosted by Washburn and that Tesson had shot Washburn as he advanced. The bullet entered Washburn's mouth and he died from the wound; yet not a tooth had been hit or disturbed in any way and I found but one living witness besides Tesson who had attended the party, and she was a full blood Indian woman over whom the two men had quarreled.

In examining the papers, I discovered an error in the indictment which made it fatally defective. I filed the demur to it and when the case was called I pointed out the error and the court sustained the demur because the District Attorney had charged that Tesson had shot one Henry Washburn and had then and there killed the said *Tesson*.

The court ordered the defendant held for action by the grand jury. When the case was presented to the jury they found but one witness who had witnessed the quarrel and the shooting and that was the old Indian woman. The grand jury did not return an indictment and the defendant was discharged. I asked one of the jurors how it happened that they did not return an indictment and he said the old woman would only grunt in answer to questions put to her through the interpreter and that they did not consider they had enough evidence to justify the returning of an indictment.

I was paid my fee but I did not get the string of bear claws.

Excerpt from Article No. XV

I was nominated on the first ballot on the morning of May 17, 1892.

After the convention was over, the Santa Fe kindly turned the private car, which had brought a number of Topeka politicians down to Emporia to defeat me, over to my delegation and took us all back to Topeka. When we arrived, we were met at the depot by a big crowd of my friends and neighbors and the delegation and I were driven to the corner of 6th and Kansas Avenue where a great reception awaited us. I was so affected by the reception that I could not respond because the tears would not stop and great lumps that gathered in my throat. I was overcome with joy at the wonderful reception which was given by my friends and neighbors. Capt. J. B. Johnson kindly responded for me.

I took a few weeks to get my law office in shape and tried a few cases and then began my campaign. I visited during the summer every school district in the Fourth Congressional District of Kansas. After my first trip, I made arrangements to have the semi-weekly Kansas City Journal sent to a large list of voters in the district and for the sending of the Western Veteran, a soldier paper, to all the soldiers of the district. I did not send the Topeka Capitol because at that time it did not stand very well with the farmers of Kansas.

Before the campaign opened I had visited every section of the district and had covered some of the ground twice. I made a note of facts and names and taught myself to remember names and instances so I

Charles Curtis

could call men by name when I met them and tell them what had happened the last time we met. It was hard at first but soon became easy to recall names and places.

I remember a visit to Burlington, Kansas. On my first trip I was introduced around by O. P. Mauck and on my second trip by Hon. John B. Kennedy. We visited a number of stores and Mr. Kennedy would be unable to call a name when I would say, "I met Mr. Scott (or whoever the man might be) when I was here before." This happened three of four times in the first block when Kennedy said, "There is no use of my going around with you for you can call more of these men by name than I can." But, he covered the city with me and he had a good time trying me out on names.

On one of my preliminary trips to Osage County we were driving up to a house when I noticed a colt caught in a barbed wire fence. I got out of the buggy, went to the fence and was releasing the colt when the owner came out; after we got the colt out I introduced myself. I had handled horses for years and knew what should be done with the colt and advised the farmer what to do. Just before the end of the campaign I was billed for a speech in the town near where the farmer lived. A little before the meeting I saw him driving up and I went out to meet him, called him by name and asked about the colt. He was glad to see me and said he did not belong to my party but he was going to vote for me because I remembered him and his colt.

On one of my trips over in Woodson County I had met a very active Populist who lived at Toronto. In the fall, I was billed for a meeting at that place, there had been an afternoon meeting at another town in the county and we drove over and because of a little mishap we were late and when we arrived in Toronto supper was over at the hotel and it was thought best for some of the local candidates to talk and for me to get something to eat at a restaurant before the meeting. At the door of the restaurant I met the man in question and called him by name. He said he would like to say a few words to me before the meeting and I asked him to join me at supper; he said he would take a cup of coffee and a piece of pie. We went to the table together and after eating he said, "I was going to ask you to let me say something at the meeting, but I don't want to now. I will say though that I am ready to vote for any man who remembers one as you have me and one who will ask a man who belongs to another party to break bread with him. I will announce tonight that I intend to support you and if the Populists don't like it, I will get off the Committee." He further said that he had not been satisfied since their convention had turned down Congressman John Otis, a good Populist, and named a former Democrat as a candidate for Congress.

Excerpt from Article No. XVII

When I returned to Washington for the opening of the Congress *(in 1900)*, I remained until Congress adjourned and did not go out home for the primaries or the convention. I kept in touch with those who were looking after my campaign and gathered a list of twenty-two thousand names in the district and on the Thursday before the primaries, I mailed a letter to every one of the twenty-two thousand. This letter was delivered Monday, the day before the primary, or on Tuesday morning which was primary day. This was the first time a letter campaign had been followed in the First District. The result was wonderful; men went to the polls early, taking my letters with them and most of them voted and worked for me all day. Early on the night of the primaries the wires began to come in and they were favorable. I knew I had won.

It was a bad night. I notified the telegraph office they need not send the other messages until morning. I forgot to tell my wife and sister that I had told the office that, as the night was bad, they need not send other messages that night and they *(my wife and sister)* sat up until about one o'clock and wondered why more messages were not delivered, and in the morning, they told me what they thought of me for not telling them.

In the morning a great stack of telegrams were delivered and they contained the news that I had carried six out of the eight counties and I had won by a big vote. I had only lost Doniphan County, the home of Mr. Leland, and Nemaha County, the home of Mr. Bailey.

Excerpt from Article XIX

After Congress adjourned, I returned with my family to our home in North Topeka. I was putting in my time visiting different parts of the district and had accepted an invitation to deliver the Decoration Day address at one of the towns in the First District but was prevented from keeping the engagement because of the great flood on the Kansas River in the latter part of May and the first of June 1903.

This late after that awful disaster it is impossible to describe it. It was the most destructive flood that ever happened in Kansas. It resulted in the loss of a number of lives, drove a number of people insane and resulted in the loss and destruction of property valued at many millions of dollars. It caused many of the oldest settlers and largest property holders to move out of North Topeka.

About five o'clock on the morning of the day when the water reached its highest point, I was called to the phone and told that the water was in the kitchen and dining room of my grandmother's home (Permelia Curtis). She lived just a block from the river. The house had been erected in 1867 and the water had never been known to be so high since the house was built.

I put on my clothes, went to the livery barn, got a horse and buggy and went down to my grandmother's home to take her from the building. She was ninety-six years old, and yet she was not afraid, said she had seen floods on the Wabash, but when told that the water was a foot or more deep in the kitchen and dining room, she concluded she would go to my sister's, Mrs. Elizabeth Colvin, for the day and night but

Charles Curtis

I had to promise I would take her back as soon as the water went down. I took her there and left her. By the time breakfast was over the water was in the streets north of the railroad which was about two and a half blocks from the river.

None of us thought it could rise much higher. When it got up to the first step leading up to our porch, I 'phoned over to the Weather Bureau and was told the river would not rise more than a foot and a half. We were all out on the porch watching the water slowly rise and our neighbors going by all seeming to enjoy the wading. We felt perfectly safe because it was still five feet to the first floor.

While we were waiting and considering what to do next, we heard an awful sound and on looking in the direction from which the noise came we saw the water pouring into a hole at the side of the basement wall under what was about the center of the dining room. I thought the foundation had given in and at once phoned for a carriage to take the family over to the south side. When the carriage came, we locked the doors of the house and left things just as they were. When we got in the carriage the water was running through the doors on either side.

We went over to the home of Charles Allen Mills, near Tenth and Topeka Avenue. I went down to the river to do what I could in helping get my neighbors over and located. We found in the morning that the water had risen about eleven feet that night. I sent a boat for my sister and her family and for my grandmother whom I had taken to my sister's the day before; when they arrived at the home, they rowed the boat in the front door and lifted my grandmother, sister and her family over the bannister of the second floor and put them in the boat.

All that day and night we were rescuing people from their homes and some from trees and tops of buildings. To add to our worries, the lime in one of the lumber yards set the lumber on fire; this drifted against some of the houses and set them on fire and there were all kind of reports as to the fire and the damage it was doing. My father-in-law and his wife were not rescued until the second day.

The people of the south side all turned out to help. Committees were formed, boats were secured and one end of the bridge had been taken out and a cable put up. No people ever did more to help those in

Racing: Indian Style

distress than did the people of South Topeka. They freely, gladly and quickly did all they could for the people in the flood district of North Topeka. Those that could not be brought over the first night were taken to the fire station and to churches and other places of safety. We kept a crowd busy sending over bread, cooked meat and fresh water and with one load I sent some quinine, tobacco, cigars and etc. to those in the fire station and they sent back a vote of thanks. There was a slow drizzling rain and most of the people had been put in the various places with their wet clothes and they were in bad shape.

    In the morning I went over to see about the damage done by the fire and to find the conditions out first hand and to pick up any whom we might find. We went up the river about one mile and then crossed over; the water was so swift in the streets that with two strong men at the oars we were carried down the street more than half a block while crossing the sixty foot. We rowed up under our porch and I got on its top and went in the house through an upstairs window.

    The water had fallen about one half an inch. It happened to be just below one of the steps and there was at least a quarter of an inch of dirt and sediment settled on the steps that had been covered by a half inch of water. I knew from that what it meant to the floors and arranged for a number of men to go in the home before the water was down to the floors and with shovels and brooms, they were able to get most of the dust and sediment off the floors by the time the water fell below.

    The clock on the mantle had stopped at 11:20 and you could see where the water had reached. It measured six feet two inches from the floor. There was a five-foot foundation from the floor to the ground which made eleven feet and two inches of water around the house.

    The people were weeks getting back into their houses and the damage was so great, the destruction of furniture, rugs and keepsakes was so awful that the people were sick and greatly discouraged and almost ready to give their property away. To stop a real estate panic, I bought all the places that were offered and stopped the selling. After a day or two, people would come to me and want to buy their house back and I sold them back at just what I had paid for them with the understanding that they wanted to move into them and would repair their homes and live in the houses. All the places I bought, except five, were taken back under those conditions.

Charles Curtis

    The damage was so great and the demands for houses to rent was so small that for fourteen years houses on the north side would not rent for enough to keep them in proper repair and pay the taxes. For three or four years after the flood of 1903, the high water was a source of great annoyance to those who lived on the north side and many sold their houses because they did not feel their families could stand the strain.

Excerpt from Article No. XX

Upon the convening of Congress in 1907, it was found that some legislation had been passed in regard to the absentee or Mexican Kickapoos (more often called the Kicking Kickapoos). These Indians owned valuable lands around Shawnee, Oklahoma but they were in Mexico most of the time and they desired to sell their lands in Oklahoma and buy a large tract of land in common in Mexico.

When the provision, which I thought was an error to pass, became a law certain parties in Oklahoma - bankers, speculators and others - joined to get ahold of the lands belonging to the Indians in Oklahoma. They sent their agents, some of whom were unscrupulous, to Mexico to get deeds and they used all kinds of tricks and resorted to questionable methods to get the Indians to sign; perjury, forgery, bribery and there was strong evidence of murder having been committed in order to secure the deeds and destroy the evidence of their doings.

A committee of the Senate consisting of Senators Teller, LaFollette and me were appointed to make an investigation. The committee went to work at once and after the first day I was asked to conduct an examination of witnesses. I wrote the report for the committee.

As a result of the investigation and report, a number of indictments were returned in Texas, but the then Governor of Oklahoma refused to grant the requisitions. Some of the land was recovered and at last a settlement was reached whereby $250,000.00 was recovered for the Indians. They are now living in Mexico- they have a fine tract of land, plenty of game and water and are able to raise good crops.

Excerpt from Article No. XXII

The treatment I received at the Kansas Day dinner, January 29, 1914, shows how a man in public life is treated after he has been retired from office. For twenty odd years, yes, from the organization of the Kansas Day Club up to and including January 29, 1913, I had always been given a place at the head table, but in 1914 I was an ex-Senator. The head table with its guests of honor and with a chairman who had been elected by my friends was there, but there was no place for an ex-Senator.

I was down with the others who had not received such recognition as would entitle them to sit at the head table, but I was happy with them and they gave me the glad hand all around. In 1915, I was again placed at the head table. I had "come back."

It all reminded me of the play *The Great Lover*. I witnessed it in New York. The leading part was that of a great singer. His reception room was always full. After each performance, great crowds came to pay him honor. He was always showered with flowers and dainty notes. But one night, his voice broke and the next night his understudy took his place. That night none stopped to pay their respects. No flowers came and friends forgot to write. There were none to do him honor and only the old servants remained true and faithful.

Sometimes, I have thought that the life of a public servant is much like that. Not quite so bad because their followers do not leave them quite so quickly. But, all but a very few of the true, tried and faithful soon forget and are applauding the new man.

About the Author

CHARLES CURTIS UNITED STATES SENATOR

Charles Curtis, United States Senator from Kansas, was born January 25, 1860, in what is now North Topeka, on the land that was allotted to his grandmother, Julie Gonville Pappan. She was a member of the Kansas tribe of Indians and was one half Indian. His great, great grandfather on his Mother's side was White Plume, Chief of the Kansas Tribe of Indian and his great, great, great grandfather on his Mother's side was Pawhuska, Chief of the Osage Tribe of Indians. His grandfather on his Mother's side was Louis Pappan, Canadian Frenchman who came among the Kansas Tribe of Indians a fur Trader. His grandfather William Curtis was born in New York. His people came from England in 1631. His grandmother Permelia Hubbard Curtis was born in New Hampshire. Her people came over on the good ship Elizabeth in 1631.

His parents were among the earliest settlers of Kansas. His father, Captain O. A. Curtis, a native of Indiana moved to Kansas in 1856; his Mother Ellen Pappan was the youngest daughter of Louis and Julie Pappan. At the age of three years, his mother died and he then lived with his father's people, Mr. and Mrs. William Curtis until he was six **(missing text)** people at the Kansas Indian Reservation in Morris County, Kansas remaining there attending the Indian Mission until 1868, the date of the Cheyenne raid, when he returned to Topeka and afterward lived with his father's parents.

(missing text) it was arranged that he should go to Indian Ter-

Charles Curtis

ritory with his maternal grandparents. But, his grandmother Pappan, who was a wonderfully bright woman, talked with him one night while camped about six miles from Topeka and told him if he ever wanted to make anything of himself, he should go back to Topeka where they had good schools and advantages and following her advice he returned to Topeka and back to school.

When a boy he was remarkable for his *(missing text)* and when not engaged with his books he was often seen selling *(missing text)* at the trains and working at the stores to help pay his school expenses. When he was eight years of age, he began riding running horses, and was a jockey during the Spring, Summer and Fall months, until 1876. That year he had arranged for a Winter contract for riding, which meant giving up school, but his Grandmother Permelia Curtis, who was always kind and dear to him, and anxious for his advancement, advised him against it, telling him if he expected to amount to anything he should give up riding and finish his education, which he did, getting all he could in the common schools of Topeka. He had the rights of majority conferred upon him at the age of nineteen, by the District Court.

He evinced a desire to improve himself intellectually and spent many of his leisure hours in hard study. His many friends of North Topeka discerned the promise of the boy and took more than ordinary interest in his welfare, and to them, and his grandmothers, Mrs. Permelia Curtis and Mrs. Julie Pappan, and his teachers, he has given much of the credit of his success.

By reason of his connection with the North Topeka Times in 1877-78-79, he made acquaintances in every part of Shawnee County. In 1879 he began the study of law in the office of A. H. Case, Esq., who was at that time and for years a leading Attorney in Kansas, he was examined and admitted to the bar of the District Court of Shawnee County in 1881, when he was twenty-one years of age. He was afterward admitted to practice in the Supreme Court of the State, and the United States District and Circuit Courts, and the Supreme Court of the United States. He was taken into partnership by Mr. Case. Being thrown to a great degree upon his own resources, he thus attained one of the chief essentials - self-reliance. He at once took high rank in the practice of his profession and was more than successful in the cases entrusted to him. He began to take part in politics soon after he began the study of law, and in 1884, was elected Prosecuting Attorney for Shawnee County, as a Republican.

He was opposed by many on account of his youth but his habits of industry and systematic work won their respect, and he demonstrated his ability to fill the office with credit to himself and his party. He was re-elected as a Republican in 1886.

His record as County Attorney is one that will long be remembered by the citizens of his state. He began to rigidly enforce the laws, and his success as a prosecutor was an agreeable surprise to his many friends. He lost only three cases during the first year, one during the second year, and none during the third or fourth year of his attorney ship.
His record as County Attorney gave him a reputation over the State, and in 1888 he was assigned as one of the speakers to fill the appointments of Honorable Thomas Ryan, in the Fourth Kansas District. After his term of office expired, he began the practice of his profession and was highly successful. In the ten years he was in active practice of the law he was engaged in the defense or prosecution of twenty-eight men who were tried for murder.

In 1892, he was elected a member of the 53rd Congress, as a Republican. He displayed his usual ability and zeal in this important office. He was always found working in the interest of the state and the people he had the honor to represent, and he won the friendship and respect of many members of that distinguished body. As a reward for his services and a proof of the appreciation of his constituents, upon his arrival home from Washington he was tendered one of the largest receptions ever given a public man in Kansas.
In November, 1894, he was reelected to Congress by an increased majority. It is said that he is personally acquainted with more people in the Fourth District than any man who has ever before represented it. He was reelected to Congress from the Fourth District in 1896. In 1897, he was legislated out to the old Fourth District and placed in the First District, and he was nominated for Congress in the First District in 1898, on the seven hundred and tenth ballot and was reelected to Congress from the First District in 1900, 1902, 1904 and 1906. While a member of the House he was on a number of important Committees among this the Ways and Means, Public Lands, Indian Affairs and others.
He was elected to the United States Senate in 1907 and received the popular vote for the Republican nomination in 1912 but was defeated under the District plan - this plan was changed by the Legislature in 1912 and in 1914 he defeated Senator Bristow for the Republican nomination

Charles Curtis

and was elected to the Senate that year and was reelected in 1920. Since he has been in Congress, he has paid strict attention to legislation of interest to the nation as a whole, as well as to the people of the State he represents. He was one of the first to take a stand for the Suffrage Amendment and has constantly done what he could to help women secure legislation beneficial to themselves and those whom were interested. He handled the Anti-Narcotic Act on the Floor of the Senate; introduced the bill for the Protection of American Women Who Marry Foreigners and at the request of representative organizations, introduced a bill for a Federal Home for United States Women Prisoners.

He was one of the first men in Congress to introduce a bill to amend the Interstate Commerce Act so as to protect the farmer. Through his efforts, with others, the wheat producers of the several states suffering from successive crop failures were assisted; he helped prepare some and was consulted in regard to nearly all the farm measures which were introduced in the last Congress and introduced the bill for Farm Loan Board allowing the Government to buy fifty million dollars of their bonds which enabled reduction of interest rates to farmers. He has been active in the support of every measure that has been of interest to the farmers and producers of the country. He introduced a bill to place agricultural industry on a sound commercial basis, to encourage Agricultural Cooperative Associations, known as the Inter State Cooperative Farm Measure. He was one of the men consulted by President Taft when what is known as the Hepburn Railroad Bill, which did away with a lot of discriminations, was passed.

He reached the conclusion, early in his career, that a bill was more likely to receive favorable action if introduced by a member of the committee having charge of the legislation, and since then he had gotten behind the measures introduced by members of committees, believing it the surest way to secure needed legislation.

He has constantly advocated amendment to the Rules of the Senate, so as to prevent filibustering and to allow the Senate to do business, instead of taking up so much time in debate. The rules were also amended as a result of a resolution he introduced, so as to permit two thirds of the Senate to close debate under certain conditions. It was upon his motion that the rules were studied so as to prevent conferees from legislating. This has virtually eliminated jokers from Acts of Congress.

It was a proposition of his that was adopted to authorize the President to consolidate Ports of Entry, which saved the taxpayers over three hundred thousand dollars a year and is saving *(more)* than that much now. He offered the amendments of the Farm Bloc to the last Revenue Bill and offered some of the amendments of the Farm Tariff Bloc to the Tariff Bill. Through his efforts, farm legislation has been taken up in the Senate as soon as possible after being reported. He has always been in favor of fully protecting the products of the farmer and the stock grower. It was largely through his efforts that amendments were adopted to various tariff bills, to protect their interests. One of his friends, in looking over the records, figured that by reason of the bills and amendments proposed by Senator Curtis which have been successful, the Government had actually saved over eighty-three million dollars.

Senator Curtis was one of the first to stand for the development of the West. It was his amendments to the Free Homes bill, that secured the passage of the Free Homes Bill for Oklahoma and other States, and with a native loyalty he has always stood for and supported all measures of benefit to that section of the country. He believes when a man goes to Congress he should come as nearly as possible representing the people of his state, but in the enactment of national legislation he should favor such measures as he thinks best for the whole country. It was his amendment that made all the Indians of the United States citizens of the United States.

The last few years he was a member of the House of Representatives, he served as Assistant Whip of that body. After entering the Senate in 1907, he was made Assistant to Senator Crane, who was then Republican Whip of the Senate, and upon his retirement in 1911, Senator Curtis was selected as Whip, serving in that capacity until March 4, 1913 when his term expired. Upon his return to the Senate in 1916, he was again made Republican Whip and Assistant Floor Leader.

He is Chairman of the Committee of Rules, and is a member of the Committee on Finance, the Committee on Appropriations, the Committee on Indian Affairs, the Committee on Committees, and the Steering Committee. This is more important Committee assignments in the Senate than any Senator has ever before held at one time. He was elected Floor Leader of the Senate by the Republican Conference in December 1924.

He was married to Annie E. Baird, eldest daughter of Mr. and Mrs. John M. Baird of North Topeka, Kansas, in 1884, a graduate of the

Charles Curtis

Topeka High School, and a most estimable young lady. There are three children - a son and two daughters all married. Mrs. Curtis was an invalid for over eight years and was helpless the last two years before her death. Since the death of Mrs. Curtis while in Topeka he makes his home with his sister and brother-in-law Mr. and Mrs. Colvin, they live in his home 1101 Topeka Ave., in that city. His sister Mrs. Edward E. Gann, formerly Miss Dolly Curtis is his hostess in Washington D. C. and when in Washington he makes his home with Mr. & Mrs. Gann. He was nominated for Vice President on the Republican ticket June 15th 1928.

Index

Concepts

15th Kansas Calvary	7
An Old Irish Cure for the Chills and Fever	53
Arrival of Freedmen in Topeka, Kansas	61
Australian Ballot	66
Awaiting Election Results	75, 129
Cheyenne Raid of the Kanza people in June, 1868	12
Claiming the Right to Majority	60
Crossing the Red River in about 1870	40
Daily Life in Early Kansas, 1860s	7, 42
Driving a Hack for Paying Customers	58
Early Physician in Topeka, Kansas	10
Ethan Allen, a Great Horse	23
First Tailored Suit	62
Government Cattle Issue to the Kanza People	11
Grand Army Lapel Pins, Copperheads and Union Soldiers	111
Gypsies and Fortune Tellers	86, 121
Hard Winter, Grasshoppers and Drought of 1873-1874	12
Immigration to New England	4
Kanza Nation Origin	1
Kanza People Travel Back to Kansas to Collect Rations	51
Kaw Mile Four, Pappan's Ferry	4, 8
Last Big Payment to the Citizens Band of Potawatomi	22
Last Wagonload of Buffalo Meat to be brought to Topeka, Kansas	11, 47
Life with the Kanza tribe near Council Grove, Kansas	11

Charles Curtis

Murder Trials	81, 84, 95, 113, 122, 135
Osage Nation Origination	1
Performing at the Opera House	61
Populist Party	103
Postmasters Chosen by Political Parties	45, 111
Potawatomie Nation	8, 22
Prohibition	66, 71, 78, 80, 88
Quaker Mission School on Kanza land at Council Grove, Kansas	11
Reflecting on a Lifetime in Politics	137
Selling Apples and Oranges at the Train Depots	45, 57
Teacher Stops the Bullying	58
Texas Long Horns	11, 20
The Curtis House (Hotel) in North Topeka (Eugene), Kansas	9, 11, 15
The Killing of Sam Wood	113
The Topeka, Kansas Flood of June, 1903	129
Topeka Republican Flambeau Club 1880	65
Traveling by Train	61, 107, 111, 119
Unethical Lawyers	64
Using the United States Mails with Intent to Defraud	122

Racing: Indian Style

Places

Kansas

Abilene	64
Auburn	96-7
Baxter Springs	25, 42
Belleville	95
Big Soldier Creek	8
Burlingame	107
Burlington	126
Butler County	111
Concordia	107-8
Council Grove	4, 13-4, 48-50
El Dorado	111
Ellsworth	19-21
Emporia	53-4, 125
Eugene (also see North Topeka)	8-11
Flint Hills	111
Fort Harker	19
Fort Riley	17
Herrington	114
Hugoton	114
Independence	1, 24-5
Indianola	8-9
Junction City	19
Kansas City	1, 21, 23, 25, 43, 53, 55-6, 122, 125
Kaw Mile Four	4, 8
Lawrence	21, 61
Leavenworth	43
Liberal	114, 116, 119
Little Soldier Creek	51
Louisville	47-8
Lux School House	72
Medicine Lodge	103
Mount Florence	7
Muscotah	63
North Topeka (also see Topeka)	4, 8-10, 16, 41-2, 45, 69, 75, 87, 105, 129-34 137
Olathe	15
Osage County	106-7, 126
Ozawkie	8
Pappan's Ferry	5, 7
Pawnee Rock	19
Phillipsburg	100-1

147

Charles Curtis

Quaker Mission School	11
Republic County	71
Rosalia	111
Rossville	104-5
Salina	52, 53-4
Santa Fe Trail	14
Shawnee County	13, 15, 66, 71, 77, 80, 95, 99-101
Silver Lake	51
Solomon	19
St. Mary's	21-3, 98
Stevens County	119-20
Territorial Capitol	17
Topeka	12-5, 17, 21, 37, 42-4, 47, 50-2, 55-6, 59, 61, 63, 65-7, 70, 72, 76-7, 79, 81, 87-8, 95, 98-100, 103-5, 107-8, 114, 122, 125, 129-34, 137
Toronto	126
Wakarusa	51, 72
Waverly	106
Wichita	48-50, 103, 114
Woodson County	126

Oklahoma (also referred to as Indian Territory)

Cherokee Nation	25, 41
Choctaw Country	41
Fort Gibson	27, 41
Krebs	41
McAlester	28
Miami	25-6
Osage County	2
Pawhuska	2
Quapaw Country	25
Shawnee	139
Stringtown	28-9, 40

Texas

Brazos River	30
Denison	39-40
Fort Worth	38
Gainesville	36-7
McKinney	29
Red River	40
San Antonio	32
Sherman	29
Texarkana	29

Waco	30-32	

Other Places

Arkansas, Fort Smith	26
Arkansas, Pine Bluffs	40
Indiana, Vermillion County	4, 5
Iowa, Des Moines	122
Pennsylvania, Philadelphia	56
Missouri, St. Louis	4, 122

Charles Curtis

People

Anderson, Mr. (livery stable keeper)	50
Anderson, Mr. (the gambler)	39
Bailey, W. J. (Honorable) (of Nemaha County)	133
Baker, William	103
Blue, James (Lawyer)	87-8
Bond, William (of Rossville)	104-5
Bond, John (of Rossville)	104-5
Botkin, Judge	114
Brennan, James	113, 115, 119-20
Bristow, Senator	145
Broderick, Case (Congressman)	103
Brown, Mr. (Mayor of Concordia)	107-8
Burnett, Abram	9
Campbell, M. T.	63, 69-70
Case, A. H. (Attorney)	59-65, 76-7, 84-6, 121
Charles, Kaw	10
Clover, Ben (Populist Leader)	103
Colvin, Elizabeth (Curtis) (sister)	5, 7, 60-3
Cooper and Darnell	47, 49
Cox, Reverend (of Salina)	54
Cozine, Mrs. (of Auburn)	96
Crumrine, Mr.	69-71
Curtis, Elizabeth (sister) see Colvin, Elizabeth	
Curtis, William (paternal grandfather)	5, 7, 11, 15-7, 42
Curtis, Permelia (paternal grandmother)	4-5, 7, 11, 15, 42, 56, 129, 135
Curtis, Ira (uncle)	42
Curtis, Annie E. (Baird) (wife)	75
Curtis, Helene (Pappan) (mother)	4-5
Davis, John (Populist Leader)	103
Dick, Thomas C. (teacher)	58
Diggs, Mrs. (Populist Leader)	103
Elliott, M. F. (Honorable)	113
Funston, E. H.	103
Garver, John (Judge) (of Waverly)	106
Gilman, Phil	16-7
Guthrie, John (Judge)	76, 79, 100
Hall, Tom (Cherokee Freedman)	41-2
Hallowell, W. L. (Prince Hall) (Populist Leader)	103
Harr, Jim	45
Harrison, President Benjamin	104, 111
Harvey, Colonel (Financial School)	106

Hudson, Jeff (Populist Leader)	103
Huffaker, Mr.	15
Humphrey, Governor	100, 106-7
Ingalls, Senator John J.	66, 103-4, 112
Ives, Attorney General	114-16
James Boys	23
Jay, Lucy (stepmother)	15
Jennison, Colonel	43
Johnson, Judge (of Council Grove)	48
Johnson, Mrs. (the clairvoyant)	121-22
Johnson, Captain J. B.	81, 125
Jones, J. W.	97
Kennedy, Vallance W.	95-6
Kennedy, John B. (of Burlington)	126
LaFollette, Bob (Senator)	139
Lamaster, Dan	43-4
Lane, Jim	65
LaTourette, Charles (uncle)	43
Lease, Mary Ellen (Populist Leader)	103
Leland, Cyrus	133
Logan, General John A.	105
Martin, Judge John	76, 78
Mauck, O. P. (of Burlington)	126
McClease, Dr.	10
McDonald, Mr. (storekeeper)	45
Mecham, Mrs.	44
Metsker, D. C.	66-70
Miller, Mayor	68
Mills, Charles Allen	130, 136
Morehouse, George P. (author)	15
Mulvane, Joab	68
Ogee, Louis (Citizen Band of Potawatomi)	10
Otis, John G. (Populist Leader)	103
Overmyer, Dave	76
Pappan, Louis (maternal grandfather)	4-5, 11, 13, 48, 51
Pappan, Julia (Gonvil) (maternal grandmother)	5, 8, 11, 13, 48, 51
Pawhuska	2, 4
Peck, Colonel George R.	67
Peffer, Judge William A.	103-4
Peters, Samuel R. (Judge)	113
Pitzer, J. N. (Attorney)	114
Ryan, Thomas (Congressman)	101
Search, Charles	52-4, 56-7
Sheldon, Dr. S. E.	71-3
Sheldon, Charles (of Osage County)	107

Charles Curtis

Short, Mr. (U. S. Deputy Marshall)	115
Simpson, (Sockless) Jerry (Populist Leader)	103
Smith, Mr. and Mrs. (of Rosalia)	111-12
Snoddy, J. D. (Attorney)	114
Teller, Senator	135
Tesson, Louis (A Sioux and Fox Indian)	122-3
Tilden, Mr.	112
Travis, L. M. (livery barn owner)	52
Troutman, James A.	66-8
Vance, A. H. (Honorable)	68, 97
Wagstaff, Colonel Dan	52, 54
Wall, Judge (of Wichita)	114-5
Wallace, George (of the carriage painting trade)	59
Washburn, Henry (Sioux and Fox Indian)	122-3
Weinberger, Mr. (Restaurant and Bakery)	57
White Plume	3
Wild Bill	9
Wilson, Andrew (Cattle King of Kansas)	50-1, 55
Wood, Sam	113-17, 119-20
Young, George (Citizen Band of Potawatomi)	10

www.ingramcontent.com/pod-product-compliance
Lightning Source LLC
Chambersburg PA
CBHW021951290426
44108CB00012B/1031